A STRAIGHTFORWARD
GUIDE
TO
UNDERSTANDING AND
CONTROLLING
INHERITANCE TAX

David Marsh

www.straightforwardco.co.uk

Straightforward Guides

© Straightforward Publishing 2017

ISBN
978-1-84716-719-4

Printed by 4Edge Ltd www.4Edge.co.uk

Cover design by Bookworks Islington

Whilst every effort has been made to ensure that the information contained within this book is correct at the time of going to press, the author and publisher can take no responsibility for any errors and omissions contained within.

Contents

Introduction

The subject of inheritance tax is an emotive one, in that most people choose not to think about it and elect to get on with their lives instead. However, particularly as we get older, it is never quite that simple and a degree of forward planning is necessary if one is to avoid relatives and loved ones paying high levels of inheritance tax after death.

This book, updated to 2017, deals with the current debates concerning inheritance tax and the various proposals put forward by various political parties to reform it.

One area that has been affected, which will be outlined in chapter eight, is the way inheritance tax has been affected by the pension reforms of 2015. Basically, this allows people who die before the age of 75 to pass on pension pots to beneficiaries tax free and subsequent draw downs will also be tax free.

Inheritance tax is a technical and complex area, or can be. Most people have a very basic understanding of the main facts, such as the inheritance tax level and so on. The purpose of this book is to enable the reader to understand the complexities and to make informed decisions about their assets and the best way to organise these assets to avoid paying exorbitant levels of tax.

The subject of inheritance tax is approached logically. Firstly the nature of inheritance tax is outlined and also how we work out inheritance tax. Assets are then explored and placed in the context of working out inheritance tax liabilities. The practice of reserving gifts is explored and we also look at the various inheritance tax relief's available.

We look at responsibility for inheritance tax and the ways in which we can further reduce the tax burden. Finally, we look at the process of probate and the importance of making a will. Overall, the reader will gain an invaluable insight into inheritance tax and how to plan so that excessive tax is avoided.

This book deals with the law as it affects the United Kingdom, as laws affecting the Channel Islands and the Isle of Man are different.

****

Chapter 1

Explaining Inheritance Tax-General Principles

In this chapter we will be looking at the following areas:

- Definition of inheritance tax (IHT)
- The law underpinning IHT
- The concept of domicile and IHT
- The making of gifts and transfers of value
- Items excluded from IHT
- Items that attract IHT
- Exempt gifts

A definition of inheritance tax

Inheritance tax is, basically, a tax on giving before death in the form of gifts or after death through a will or through the administration of a person's affairs if a will is not left. For general purposes, anything over £325,000 (2017-2018) is payable at 40% or 36% if the estate qualifies for a reduced rate as a result of a charitable donation (if you leave mor4e than 10% of the net value of your estate). There are a number of ways to minimise inheritance tax liability as we will see.

Increased threshold for married couples and civil partners

Since October 2007, married couples and registered civil partners can effectively increase the threshold on their estate when the second partner dies - to as much as £850,000 in 2017-18. Their executors or personal representatives must transfer the first spouse or civil partner's unused Inheritance Tax threshold or 'nil rate band' to the second spouse or civil partner when they die. However, some people whose partner dies before 21st March 1972 are caught by a different law and won't benefit from the double allowance.. If you give away your home to your children (including adopted, foster or stepchildren) or grandchildren, your threshold will increase to £425,000 (from April 2017). This will rise to £500,000 (or £1m for couples) by April 2020.

The Legislation covering inheritance tax

The law governing inheritance tax is based on the Inheritance Tax Act 1984 as amended. Fundamentally, inheritance tax becomes payable after death or when there is what is known as a *transfer of value* as the result of a transfer of property (such as the making of a gift or gifts) or a failure to act, unless the transfer or failure is within one of the exemptions allowed for, which will be outlined later. In this case it is known as an exempt disposition. A transfer is also exempt if the property in respect of which the transfer takes place is an *excluded property* or *excluded gift*. The tax payable is less if the inheritance relief's specified in the Act notionally reduce either the value of the property or the tax itself.

The Concept of Domicile

Although there are other taxes, none of these are affected by domicile as is IHT (domicile or tax residence arises if the taxpayer has his or her residence in the state where he or she spends most of their time). If a taxpayer has his or her residence in the United Kingdom, or is deemed to have it there, inheritance tax is charged whenever there is a gratuitous transfer of value (other than exemptions) in respect of assets in whatever country they may be. If the taxpayer's domicile is outside the UK, the tax only applies to those assets that are situated in the UK.

A person will have his or her domicile in the state which he considers to be his permanent home, even though he might not have the right of residence there.

For inheritance tax purposes it is important to understand the nature of domicile. At birth, a person will have the domicile of his mother if he is illegitimate or his father is dead, other wise he will have the domicile of his father. A person can exchange the domicile of origin (or birth) for one of choice once over the age of 16 and mentally capable. If there is an intention to live there indefinitely, whether legally or not, then this will be deemed to be the domicile of choice. If a person is dependent on another, whether mentally incapable or under 16, this will be known as a domicile of dependency.

Deemed domicile

Deemed domicile affects those who live in the UK for a long period of time without acquiring domicile of choice here. Once one has lived in the UK for 17 out of the last 20 years, one is deemed domiciled for IHT purposes only. At this stage a non-domiciled spouse would benefit from the same IHT treatment as a fully domiciled spouse, i.e. all transfers to that spouse upon the death of their husband and wife would be exempt from IHT, but up to that point an onerous tax burden could arise.

Inheritance tax and transfers of value

The Inheritance Tax Act 1984 defines transfer of value as 'a disposition by a person, as a result of which the value of his estate immediately after the disposition is less than it would be but for the disposition; and the amount by which it is less is the 'value transferred' by the transfer'.

Deciphering this, calculation of inheritance tax is based upon the reduction the transaction causes to the wealth of the giver and not the increase in the recipients wealth.

Taxable and non-taxable giving

Some transactions which cause a reduction in the taxpayer's wealth are declared by the Act as not to be transfers of value and therefore are exempt. Section 10 of the Inheritance Tax Act 1984 states 'A disposition which is not intended…to confer any gratuitous benefit and which is either entered into at arms length between 'persons not connected with each other' or which is 'such as might be expected to be' entered into at 'arms length between persons not connected with each other' is not taxable.

Persons connected with each other for this purpose are the taxpayer's family including spouse or civil partner, ancestors, lineal descendants, brothers and sisters, uncles and aunts, nephews and nieces, the spouse or the civil partner of the above family members and the relatives in the same categories of the taxpayers spouse or civil partner.

Except in respect of commercial transactions relating to partnership assets, the taxpayer's business partner and the partners spouse or registered civil partner are also considered to be connected to him.

In addition, transfers made during the taxpayers lifetime in favour of a spouse, registered civil partner or a child of the taxpayer or child of his spouse or registered civil partner, for the purpose of family maintenance are exempt. This exemption applies not only during the subsistence of the relationship but also in respect of arrangements made on the annulment or dissolution of the relationship. It also provides for transfers for the reasonable maintenance of a dependant relative. In the case of a child it only applies to transfers of value for the maintenance, education or training of the child until he attains 18 years of age or until he ceases full time education if later.

One other exemption is the grant of an agricultural tenancy for full consideration, payable in money or moneys worth.

Property excluded from inheritance tax

Certain property (property is not limited to bricks and mortar) is not liable to incur inheritance tax as below:

- Savings Certificates and Premium bonds owned by people who are domiciled in the Channel Islands or the Isle of Man.
- Certain British Government stock owned by those living abroad.
- Certain overseas pensions and lump sums payable on death.

- Emoluments and tangible movable property which is owned by visiting armed forces.

- Property of service people who die as a result of active military service.

- By concession, decorations awarded for valour or gallantry which have never been transferred in return for money or moneys worth. The decoration need not have been solely a medal or remain in the same family.

- Property situated outside the United Kingdom which belongs to a person who is domiciled outside of the United Kingdom.

- Foreign currency bank accounts with most banks in the UK that are held by people who are of foreign domicile and who are not resident or ordinarily resident in the UK.

- Most reversionary interests, i.e. most presently owned rights to property upon the death of someone who is currently entitled to their property during their lifetime under a trust.

Assets that incur inheritance tax liability

The assets that attract inheritance tax liability (unless excluded) are as follows:

a) Everything that the taxpayer owns (including shares of property co-owned with someone else.

b) Everything that he has given away in the last seven years of his life unless they are exempted gifts

c) Every non-exempt gift he has made from which he has reserved a right to benefit in the last seven years.

d) Everything owned by someone else from which the taxpayer is entitled to benefit for the remainder of the taxpayers life or for any other limited period (known as a life tenancy) or the assets of any trust fund of which the taxpayer has a right to the income for the rest of his life, if

a) the life tenant was entitled as a disabled person under a trust   for the disabled (see chapter on trusts)

b) - the life tenancy was created by a will or intestacy and began immediately upon the death, or

c) the life tenancy was created by an arrangement or trust created before 22 March 2006, or

d) the life tenancy follows immediately upon a life tenancy in existence on April 6th 2006 that ended before April 6th 2008, or

e) the life tenant was the spouse or the civil partner of a person who was a life tenant under a pre-April 2006 trust at that date who died on or after 6th April 2008 and the life tenants entitlement immediately followed on that of his spouse or civil partner, or

f) the life tenancy is the first or a subsequent life tenancy in a trust created before 22nd March 2006 which is a trust of a life policy or life policies, provided that there has been no break in the sequence of life tenancies.

a, b and c above are known as the taxpayer's free estate and 4 as the settled estate.

From the total of these assets it is permissible to deduct the debts and financial liabilities transferred with the assets to which they relate and if the transfer of value takes place as a result of the taxpayer's death, the amount of the taxpayer's debts and reasonable funeral expenses.

However, if the taxpayer is insolvent it is not allowed to deduct any deficiency in the free estate from the settled estate.

Gifts that are exempt

Gifts that are exempt from inheritance tax are the following:

- Gifts made by the taxpayer more than seven years prior to his death without retaining any benefit from the gift, unless the gift is made to a company or a trust (other than a trust for the disabled). These gifts are known as immediately chargeable gifts. With the exception of immediately chargeable gifts, gifts only remain potentially liable to inheritance tax for the seven years after they have been made and are known as PET's (Potentially exempt transfers). If the donor survives the making of a PET by seven years the PET is exempt from IT. Gifts that count as a PET are gifts that you, as an individual, make to another individual, a trust for someone who is disabled or a bereaved minor's trust. This is where, as the beneficiary of an Interest in possession Trust you decide to give up the right to receive anything from that trust or that right comes to an end for any other reason during your lifetime. See chapter on trusts.
- Gifts of any amount to a spouse or civil partner, unless the taxpayer is domiciled in the UK, but the spouse or civil partner is not, in which case the exemption is limited to £55,000.

- Gifts of not more than £3000 in total made in any tax year during the lifetime of the taxpayer. Any unused benefit from this exemption can be carried forward for one tax year and the annual exemption for any current tax year is used up before the unused balance of the annual exemption from any previous tax year.

- Gifts made during the taxpayer's lifetime which are made as part of the normal expenditure of the taxpayer out of his income and not from capital and which do not reduce his standard of living. Normal expenditure is expenditure which is in accordance with a settled pattern of the donor's expenditure.

- Wedding gifts made before the ceremony during the taxpayer's lifetime, up to £5,000 to his child, up to £2,500 to his grandchild and up to £1000 in the case of anyone else.

- Gifts made in the taxpayer's lifetime for the maintenance of a spouse, ex spouse, civil partner, ex civil partner, dependant relatives and dependant children who are under the age of 18 or are in full time education.

- Gifts to registered charities for charitable purposes.

- Gifts for certain national purposes including gifts to most museums and art galleries and to political parties which have at least two sitting members of the House of Commons or which have one sitting member and whose candidate polled 150,000 votes at the next general election.

- Gifts of land to registered housing associations.

Gifts in any number of the above classes can be made to the same person without losing the benefit of the exemption and under the small gifts exemption any number of gifts up to £250 can be made in a tax year provided that no other gift has been made to the same person in the same tax year. If the sum given under the small gifts exemption exceeds £250 the benefit of the exemption is lost and the entire amount is taxable.

Married people and those with registered civil partners should remember that each spouse and civil partner has a separate set of gift exemptions.

The percentage of the value of any gift which is not an exempt disposition or gift of excluded property that is extracted as tax, i.e. the rate of tax charged, is dependent upon whether the gift is deemed to have been made at the time of the taxpayers death or whether it was made during his life and if so how long he survived the making of the gift. It also depends on who or what organisation was the recipient of the gift and the type of property given. It is therefore essential to ensure that full documentary evidence which shows dates and value of all gifts is kept, plus when they were made.

****

Chapter 2

Inheritance Tax Calculation

In this chapter we look at the following:

- The IHT tax threshold
- Calculation of IHT payable on gifts in life
- Calculation of IHT on gifts in death
- Immediately chargeable lifetime gifts

Each year the government creates a tax threshold, which is a sum below which no inheritance tax is payable. Currently in 2017/2018 this is £325,000. Therefore, if your estate is less than this amount no tax will be payable. The band below £325,000 is known as the nil-rate band. The rate applicable to lifetime chargeable transfers in excess of the nil-rate band is 20% and the rate applicable to chargeable transfers on death above the nil-rate band is 40%.

If you give away your home to your children (including adopted, foster or stepchildren) or grandchildren, your threshold will increase to £425,000 and rise to £500,000 by 2020.

If you're married or in a civil partnership and your estate is worth less than your threshold, any unused threshold can be added to your partner's threshold when you die. This means their threshold can be as much as £850,000.

As we have mentioned, gifts and transfers of value are valued for inheritance tax purposes at the amount by which the estate of the person making the transfer is diminished as a result of the transfer and not by the amount by which the recipient or any other person benefits from the transfer.

Inheritance tax on gifts in life

To calculate the amount of inheritance tax payable on a gift made during life you should:

1. total all the chargeable transfers of value made by the giver within the previous seven tax years excluding any exempt gifts and excluded property
2. deduct any debts and financial liabilities which are transferred with the asset to which the debt or financial liability relates
3. deduct the balance of the tax threshold which remains unused by previous non-exempt gifts made in the previous seven years
4. apply the full lifetime rate of tax to the resultant figure
5. if the transfer was made more than three years before death, apply taper relief to the amount of tax (see further on in the book)

Inheritance tax payable on death

To calculate IT payable on the estate following death, add the total of the net death estate to the total of the chargeable lifetime gifts made in the previous seven years and deduct any balance of the tax threshold which has not been used in respect of lifetime gifts. Apply the full death tax rate to this figure and then deduct the full tax payable on the lifetime gifts. There are permissible deductions when calculating the net estate on death:

- any legacies which are exempt gifts, e.g. legacies to a spouse or to a registered charity for its charitable purposes
- reasonable funeral and mourning expenses including the cost of a memorial
- any debts and liabilities existing at the date of death for which the taxpayer had received value or that were imposed by law, e.g. outstanding income tax
- the cost of realising or administering any property which is situated outside the United Kingdom up to 50% of its value
- excluded property.

Calculating the nil-rate band which remains available on death
Any non-exempt gift (other than excluded property) made in the seven years before a death is deducted from the tax exemption threshold available to be set against the net estate at death by the value transferred by the gift.

Calculating the nil-rate band when making an immediately chargeable lifetime gift.
When dealing with immediately chargeable lifetime gifts (gifts made during life to trusts, other than trusts for the benefit of disabled beneficiaries or to companies), to calculate the value of the inheritance tax exemption threshold which can be set against the gift, it is necessary to deduct from the then current IT threshold figure the total value of all immediately chargeable gifts made by the

giver in the last seven years. If the total value of the immediately chargeable gifts made in the previous seven years and the current gift exceeds the current tax threshold, tax is payable on the excess. Gifts other than immediately chargeable gifts are ignored and are not deducted from the threshold figure when calculating how much of the nil-rate band remains and is available to set off against an immediately chargeable gift, because being PET's, they are still potentially exempt and not chargeable.

Gifts are treated as being deducted in chronological order in which they are made. For example if a gift of £200,000 is made two years before death to A and one year later £200,000 is gifted to B the gift to A will be exempt from tax but B may well be charged tax, depending on the amount of threshold at the date of death.

If the total value of immediately chargeable non- exempt gifts made in the previous seven years and the value of the immediately chargeable gift currently being made exceeds the then tax threshold, inheritance tax (at one half the rate in respect of gifts made on death) is immediately payable on the excess. Credit is given on death for tax that has been paid on immediately chargeable gifts made in the previous seven years, but if the tax paid exceeds the tax payable on them at death the excess is not repayable.

As has been previously outlined, transfers made more than seven years before death are exempt transfers. Transfers made in the seven years immediately preceding death are potentially exempt until death occurs, unless they are immediately chargeable gifts. Transfers other than immediately chargeable transfers are not taken into account when calculating the tax payable on immediately chargeable transfers until death occurs when a revision of the tax might or might not become necessary, depending how long has elapsed between the transfer and death.

****

Chapter 3

Valuing Assets

In this chapter we cover the following:

- The calculation of asset value
- Grossing up profits

Calculating assets

We will also cover this area in the final chapters of the book when dealing with probate.

Assets are valued for the purposes of IHT at their open market value. Rules exist to assist HMRC in valuing assets.

Valuation of unit trusts, corporate bonds and other stock

As is well known, unit trusts have two values, one at which managers are willing to sell units and the lower price at which managers are willing to buy them back. For IT purposes, unit trusts are valued at the lower of the prices.

Corporate bonds and other stock also have a buying price and a lower selling price. The taxpayer can choose which of these two figures he will use, as opposed to HMRC. Valuations of stocks and shares for IT purposes can be obtained from most banks and stockbrokers or from www.sharedata.co.uk and there is a charge for this information.

If a share has been quoted 'ex-dividend' the dividend which has been declared must be included in the valuation for inheritance tax purposes: if debenture or loan stock is quoted ex-interest, the interest (less tax at the appropriate rate) must be included.

Stocks and shares that are not quoted

The basis upon which stocks and shares that are not quoted on a recognised stock exchange are valued will depend on the percentage of the company's share capital held by the taxpayer. A Shareholding of 50% or less is valued according to the dividend yield. A holding of between 50% and 90% on an earnings yield and a holding of 90% or over on an asset basis.

Life policies

If the life policy is valued at the time of death the value is the sum paid out by the assurance company. If the transfer occurs on any other occasion the value is the open market value at which the policy could be sold (not the surrender value).

Property that is related

Related property is property which would have an increased value if owned with other property that is:

- owned by the taxpayers spouse or civil partner, or
- was owned within the last five years by a charity, housing authority, political party which qualifies for exempt transfers or an institution in the amended schedule 3 of the Inheritance Tax Act 1986, to which it was transferred by the taxpayer or his spouse or civil partner after April 15th 1976.

There are two methods of valuing related property-the general method and the special rule method. The general rule method is used when items of related property have different attributes. The special method is used when property has identical attributes.

Land, shares, and other sold within a short time of death

If the value of shares (other than those quoted on the Alternative Investment market AIM), unit trusts, common investment funds and land or buildings fall during the period of administration of an estate, and in the course of the administration they are sold to a beneficiary at a loss, compared to their value at the date of death, then it is perfectly reasonable to have the value revised to reflect the fall. This reduced value will also become the base cost for capital gains purposes.

To obtain an agreement by HMRC to a revaluation in the case of stock exchange securities and unit trusts, the personal representatives must have sold them within 12 months of the date of death. If the personal representatives reinvest the proceeds of sale by buying further unit trusts or quoted investments within two months of the last sale during the 12-month period, the amount of repayable tax will be restricted.

Similar principles apply in the case of land or buildings, the main difference being that the period of sale is four years instead of 12 months.

The period for reinvestment is four months after the last qualifying sale in the period of four years from death instead of two moths during the period of 12 months from death and sales at a profit in the fourth year after death or which result in a profit or loss of less than 5% or £1,000 whichever is the lower, are ignored.

Grossing up gifts

Inheritance tax payable on immediately chargeable lifetime gifts is payable by the donor unless agreed otherwise. If the tax is paid by the donor the gift must be 'grossed up' for the purpose of calculating inheritance tax. This means that the gift is considered to be the amount of the gift and the tax because that is the amount by which the donors wealth has diminished. If additional tax is paid because the donor dies within seven years of making the gift, it is always paid by the donee.

Rates of inheritance tax and any allowances and exemptions can be found on HMRC website www. hmrc.gov.uk.

****

Chapter 4

The Pre-owned Assets Tax Charge

In this chapter will look at:

- The reservation of benefits
- The pre-owned assets income tax charge
- Calculation of the charge
- Exceptions to the charge

Reserving benefits

If a gift is made but a benefit is reserved by the giver, for example the continued use of a house or other property, the asset is still deemed to be part of the taxpayer's estate as long as he derives benefit from it or is entitled to benefit from it without making any payment for the use or benefit at a full commercial rate. The gift is not deemed to have been fully made until the donee takes full possession of it

Not surprisingly, HMRC takes a strict view of what exactly constitutes reservation of benefit and considers there is a reservation of benefit in any case where the benefit is significant in relation to the property given.

An example might be the use of a house that has been gifted. Once the house is gifted, HMRC would see very occasional use by the donor as not constituting a reservation but frequent use would. It is wise, in the long run, to avoid making or creating any form of reservation once property of any description is gifted.

Pre-owned assets tax charge

As might be imagined, people come up with various diverse and complicated schemes to avoid inheritance tax liability resulting from gifts with reservation. However, HMRC, as usual, is on the case. In the budget of March 2004, the then Chancellor Gordon Brown outlined proposals for what is known as the 'free standing income tax charge' based on pre-owned assets to counteract these schemes and 'the benefit that people get from having free or low cost enjoyment of assets they formerly owned or provided funds to purchase. Basically, if a scheme succeeds in the avoidance of inheritance tax liability that results from the reservation of benefit rules, then liability for income tax is likely to be incurred under the pre-owned assets charge.

The pre-owned assets charge is similar in nature to tax paid by employees for benefits in kind supplied by their employees. A financial sum is attributed to the benefit and tax is paid accordingly. Cash value benefits under £5,000 are disregarded. This law came into being from 6th April 2005 and applies to all gifts made after 17th March 1986.

The charge applies to both tangible and intangible assets. It also applies to any funds or contributions to funds used to acquire the assets from which the donor benefits and whether the funds or contributions are directly or indirectly provided. In the case of those who are deemed to domiciled in the United Kingdom, the charge applies to assets held anywhere in the world and in the case of anyone else only to their assets in the UK.

Calculating the tax charge

The amount of tax payable is a sum equivelant to the annual rental value of the asset in the case of land or buildings and in the case of other assets to a rate of interest on a notional loan of a sum equal to the market value of the asset, and in each case less any payment made under a legally binding agreement for the use of the asset. After the deduction of the amount paid for the benefit, the sum so ascertained is added to the taxpayer's taxable income and taxed at his top rate of tax. The first £5,000 per annum is ignored but once the £5,000 is exceeded the exemption is totally lost.

The current rate of interest is set out in the *Charge to income tax by Reference to Enjoyment of Property previously owned Regulations 2005* (Statutory Instrument no 724).

Exceptions

As usual there are exceptions to the above charge as follows:

- the asset ceased to be owned before March 18th 1986
- the formerly owned asset is currently owned by the taxpayer's civil partner or spouse
- the asset was transferred to a spouse, former spouse, civil partner or former civil partner by court order
- the entire asset was sold for its cash value in a transaction on arm's length terms whether or not the parties were connected persons

- the owner of the asset was formerly the owner of the asset only by virtue of a will or intestacy which has subsequently been varied by agreement between the parties, i.e. by a deed of family arrangement as explained further in the book

- the asset is land or buildings which have been given and the donor and the person to whom it is given share the occupation of the land and either the donor pays all the running costs and capital expenses relating to the occupation of the property or an amount at least proportionate to his share of the ownership and use of the property so that he cannot be said to be retaining any benefit from the arrangement

- the gift does not take the asset out of the donor's taxable estate for inheritance tax purposes. e.g. a gift to a company in which the donor owns all the shares or the asset still counts as an asset of the donor for inheritance tax purposes under the gift with a reservation rules

- any benefit is no more than incidental

- the gift is an outright gift of money used to acquire land or another asset made seven years or more before the earliest date upon which the donor either occupied the land or had the use of the asset

- the original gift was for the maintenance of the donors family or within the small gifts exemption (£250 per donee) or within the annual gift allowance (£3000 in total

- the donor is not resident in the UK

- the asset which gives rise to the benefit is situated abroad and the donor does not have his domicile in the UK

- the asset is a non-UK asset which the taxpayer ceased to own before he became domiciled in the UK
- the aggregate benefits do not exceed more than £5000 in one year.

If the taxpayer so elects before 31st January after the end of the first tax year in which the pre-owned assets rule applies to him he can choose to have the property in question treated as part of his estate for inheritance tax purposes as a gift with reservation of an interest rather than have the benefit taxed as an income. Whether it will be advantageous for a taxpayer to opt into inheritance tax by reason of the transaction being a gift with a reservation of a benefit instead of paying the pre-owned asset income tax charge will depend upon how long he has to live, the amount of the income tax charge and the rate at which his income is taxed.

If a taxpayer gives an asset away and pays a full commercial rent or hiring fee to use it, although doing so will save inheritance tax, it will not usually be an otherwise tax efficient tax efficient transaction because as far as income tax is concerned, the taxpayer will be paying the rent or hiring fee out of taxable income and the recipient of the gift will have to pay income tax on the rent. If the taxpayer's principal private residence is the subject of the transaction, the capital gains exemption for a principal private residence will be lost when the donee comes to sell the property unless during the period of the donor's benefit the donee also uses it as his principal private residence.

****

Chapter 5

The Various Inheritance Tax Relief's Available

In this chapter we cover the following:

- Various relief's available when calculating IHT
- Rates of relief
- Businesses which do not attract relief
- The minimum period of ownership
- Shares and relief
- Paying tax on business property
- Agricultural property
- Woodland relief
- Death and military service
- Deeds of family arrangement

Certain circumstances, and property, attract inheritance tax relief. The main areas are listed below.

Taper relief

In the case of gifts made between three and seven years of death, tax is charged proportionately. The proportion will depend on how long the maker of the gift survives the making of the gift. This reduction is known as taper relief.

The 7 year rule

If there's Inheritance Tax to pay, it's charged at 40% on gifts given in the 3 years before you die.

Gifts made 3 to 7 years before your death are taxed on a sliding scale known as 'taper relief'.

Years between gift and death	Tax paid
less than 3	40%
3 to 4	32%
4 to 5	24%
5 to 6	16%
6 to 7	8%
7 or more	0%

Gifts are not counted towards the value of your estate after 7 years.

Business property relief

Business relief on certain types of business can be claimed if they qualify as a relevant business property and the transferor has owned them for a minimum period. Relief can be claimed for transfers made during a person's lifetime and on death and on chargeable occasions arising on relevant business property held on trust.

Types of business property on which relief can be claimed

A person can claim business relief on:

- a business or an interest in business (such as a partner in a partnership)
- unquoted shares. This includes shares which are traded in the unlisted securities market (USM shares) or the Alternative Investment market (AIM). Shares that are listed on a recognised overseas stock exchange are quoted for IHT purposes, even if they are also traded in the AIM or USM.
- A holding of shares or securities owned by the transferor, which are fully listed on a recognised stock exchange, which themselves or with other listed shares give control of a company.
- Land, buildings, plant or machinery owned by a partner of a controlling shareholder and used wholly or mainly in the business or the partnership or company immediately before the transfer. This applies only if the partnership interest or shareholding would itself, if transferred, qualify for business relief.
- Any land, buildings machinery or plant which was used wholly or mainly for the purpose of a business carried on by a transferor and was settled property in which the transferor was beneficially entitled to an interest in possession and used in the transferor's business.

Rate of relief

If the asset qualifies for relief, the rate at which it is allowed is shown below. The relief is given by deducting the relevant percentage of the capital value of the asset. The below deals with transfers after 6th April 1996.

A business or an interest in a business   100%

A holding of shares in an unquoted company   100%

Control holding of shares in a quoted company   50%

(More than 50% of the voting rights)

Land, buildings, plant or machinery used in a business of which the deceased was a partner at the date of death or used by a company controlled by the deceased.   50%

Land, buildings or machinery held in trust where the deceased had the right to benefit from the trust and the asset was used in a business carried on by the deceased.   50%

Business on which relief cannot be claimed

Relief cannot be claimed if the:

- business or company is engaged wholly or mainly in dealing with securities, stocks or shares, land or buildings, or in making or holding investments
- business is not carried on for gain
- business is subject to a contract for sale, unless that sale is to a company which will carry on the business, and the sale is made wholly or mainly in consideration of shares in the company buying the business
- shares in the company are subject to a contract for sale or the company is being wound up, unless the sale or winding up is part of a reconstruction or amalgamation to enable the business of the company to carry on.

Relief may be available for:

- the business of a market maker or discount house in the United Kingdom
- shares or securities in a company which is a holding company and the group is not wholly or mainly engaged in property, investment or dealing.

Calculating the value of relevant business property

If business relief is being deducted at 100% from the value of the deceased's business or interest in a business, the value of the business can include the value of the business as shown in the company's accounts. If you are not deducting business relief at 100% you will have to adjust the value taken from the company's accounts to ensure that you include the open market value of the business rather than the book value. Individual assets in the business, such as land, buildings, stock, goodwill and machinery may be included at book value.

Excepted assets

Some assets are known as excepted and do not qualify for relief. An asset is excepted if it is:

- not used wholly or mainly for the purposes of the business throughout the two years immediately before the transfer (or since its acquisition by the business if more recent)
- not required at the time of the transfer for identified future use for the purpose of the business, or
- used wholly or mainly for the personal benefit of the transferor, or a person connected with the transferor (e.g. spouse, child or relative).

Shares in a holding company

Special rules apply if the relevant business property is a controlling shareholding in a holding company. If the group includes any company whose own business falls outside the scope of the relief, business relief is only given on the value that would be appropriate if that company were not part of the group. In applying the rules for excepted assets the group is treated as one concern.

The minimum period of ownership

The general rule is that property is not relevant business property (and so does not qualify for relief) unless it was owned as such by the transferor throughout the two years immediately before the transfer. There are certain points to note:

- If the transferor becomes entitled to the property on the death of a spouse or civil partner, relief is available for any period during which the spouse or civil partner owned it.
- If the transferred property was acquired on an earlier transfer within the two year period relief is available if:
- The earlier transfer was eligible for business relief
- The earlier transfer was made to the current transferor or spouse or civil partner
- One of the transfers was made on death, and
- The property, apart from the two-year rule, would qualify for relief.
- Relief is available when the transferred property replaces other relievable property
- If the transferor inherits the property on death, the ownership is considered to run from the date of death.

Business relief and a gift of business property

Business relief is only given if, or to the extent that, the gifted property:

- was relevant business property at the time that the transfer was made
- was owned by the transferee throughout the period between the gift and the death of the transferor, or the earlier death of the transferee, subject to special rules for replacement property (below)
- immediately before the transferor's death or the earlier death of the transferee, remains property eligible for relief as relevant business property.

It is available at the rate appropriate to the property at the time the gift occurred.

Part of a gift qualifying for relief

If, at the date of the transferor's death the conditions for relief are satisfied for only a part of the gifted property, a proportionate part of the value that was transferred is reduced. If the transferee dies before the transferor the conditions for relief have to be satisfied at both the date of the gift and the time of the transferor's death.

Rules for replacement property

Where the original relevant business property was disposed of before the transferor's death and the proceeds were used to buy replacement property, the relief is not necessarily lost. In order to still qualify for relief:

- the whole of the sale proceeds must have been used to purchase the replacement property and
- both the sale and the purchase must have been arm's length transactions taking place within three years of each other.

The replacement property must also be of such a nature that, if it was transferred by the transferee immediately before the death of the transferor, it would, apart from the minimum period of ownership requirement, qualify for relief.

Generally, the property is treated as satisfying the two-year ownership test if:

- it replaces other property (which may have replaced other property and so on)
- the transferor owned property in the chain for periods amounting to at least two years during the five years immediately before the transfer, and
- each item in the chain, which is taken into account for the two-year ownership period, would have been relevant business property (apart from the length of ownership) if the transfer of value had taken place immediately before the item was replaced.

Shares exchanged for other shares

Where shares are exchanged for other shares, the time of ownership of previous shares counts towards the two-year period. This can happen in a capital reorganisation or amalgamation.

Paying tax on business property

If inheritance tax is due and there is not 100% relief, business tax can be paid in instalments on:

- certain shares and securities. You may be able to pay tax in instalments if they gave the deceased control of the company at the time of the transfer or they are unquoted and either you can show that the tax attributable to their value could not be paid in one sum without undue hardship or at least 20% of the tax for which the same person is liable in the same capacity is attributable to assets that qualify for payment by instalments. In the case of unquoted shares only, their value exceeds £20,000 and the shares transferred represent at least 10% of the nominal value of the company's share capital or the ordinary share capital.

- the net value of a business or an interest in a business, including a profession or a vocation, carried on for gain (this does not include individual assets of a business, which are distinct from the business as a whole).

In certain cases, interest will be charged on instalments.

Agricultural property

Agricultural relief is available on the agricultural value of property which is transferred. The agricultural property can be owner occupied or let. Relief is only due if the transferor has owned the property and it has been occupied for agricultural purposes for a minimum period. The relief is only available if the agricultural property was either

- occupied by the transferor for agricultural purposes for the two years immediately before the transfer or
- owned by the transferor throughout the seven years immediately before the transfer and throughout that period has been occupied for agricultural purposes (whether by the transferor or by another). Additional tests have to be satisfied where a charge or increased charge to IHT arises because the transferor died within seven years of the transfer.

When is agricultural relief available?

Relief is available for transfers:

- in life
- on death, and
- when agricultural property is chargeable as settled property.

What is agricultural property?

For the purpose of the relief, agricultural property must be in the UK, Channel Islands or the Isle of Man. The term means agricultural land or pasture, but it also includes:

- any farmhouse, cottages or buildings which are of a character appropriate to the property
- woodlands or buildings used for intensive rearing of livestock, or fish, if those woodlands or buildings are occupied with agricultural land or pasture and the occupation is ancillary to that of the agricultural land or pasture (where woodlands are agricultural property they are not eligible for woodlands relief)
- growing crops, when transferred with the land

46

- stud farms engaged in the breeding and rearing of horses and land used for grazing associated with those activities
- land and buildings used in the cultivation of short rotation coppice, for transfers on or after 6th April 1995
- any land within a habitat scheme for transfers on or after 26th November 1996.

Milk quotas

Where agricultural land, or an interest in agricultural land, is valued and the valuation of the land reflects the benefit of a milk quota, agricultural relief is available on that overall value.

Agricultural value

The relief only applies to the value of the agricultural property. This is the value the property would have if it could only be used as agricultural property. The relief does not extend to any other element in the open market value of such property, for example:

- development value
- the additional value of a house as a desirable country residence.

Farmhouses and cottages

Agricultural relief is allowable on the agricultural value of farm cottages occupied for agricultural purposes with agricultural land or pasture. To qualify for relief the farm cottage must meet the conditions about the period of occupation and ownership.

If the cottage has a value over and above its agricultural value because it could be attractive as a second home, for example, that additional value will not attract agricultural relief. Normally a farm cottage or farmhouse occupied by someone who is not employed in agriculture will not qualify for relief. By concession, a cottage occupied by a retired farm employee or their widow, widower or surviving civil partner is treated as being occupied for agricultural purposes if either:

- the occupier is a statutorily protected tenant, or
- the occupation is under a lease granted to the farm employee for his or her life, and that of any surviving spouse or civil partner, as part of the employee's contract of employment by the landlord for agricultural purposes.

The rate of relief

The rate of relief is either 100% or 50%. Relief is due at 100% if:

- immediately before the transfer the transferor had the right to vacant possession of the property or the right to obtain it within the next twelve months, or
- land was let on a grazing licence
- property is let on a tenancy beginning on or after 1st September 1995, 0r
- the transitional provisions for let property apply.

Relief is due at a lower rate of 50% in any other case (principally where property is let on a tenancy granted before 1st September 1995 and the transitional provisions do not apply.

Transitional relief

In some circumstances land let on a tenancy starting before 10th March 1981 may qualify for relief at 100% on a transfer after that date. The conditions are that:

- the transferor owned the land since before 10th March 1981, and
- the land would have qualified for full agricultural relief under Schedule 8 FA 1975 had it been transferred before 10th March 1981, and
- the transferor neither had nor could have had the right to vacant possession between that date and the date of the current transfer.

Relief on mortgaged property

You should work out the part to which the relief applies if:

- the agricultural property that is transferred is subject to a mortgage or other secured liability, or
- the relief is due on only part of the property that is transferred.

Example

Mr Brown dies owning let land valued at £250,000. The rate of relief is 50%. Part is non-agricultural, and the agricultural value of the agricultural property transferred is £200,000. A mortgage of £60,000 is secured on the total property being transferred.

Item	Amount
Value of agricultural property	£200,000
Less proportion of the mortgage applicable	
To the agricultural property	
£200,000/£250,000 x £60,000	£48,000
Sub total	£152,000
Less amount of agricultural relief at 50%	£76,000
Chargeable balance after relief	£76,000
Value of non-agricultural property	£50,000
(£250,000 - £200,000)	
Less balance of mortgage	£12,000
(£60,000 - £48,000)	
Sub total	£38,000
Total value on which tax is chargeable	£114,000

Company shares and securities

Company shares and securities are treated as follows:

- their value can be attributed to the agricultural property which forms part of the company's assets, and
- they gave the transferor control of the company immediately before the transfer
- the agricultural property was:
- occupied for agricultural purposes by the company or the transferor for the two years immediately prior to the transfer, or
- owned by the company for the seven years immediately before the transfer, and
- occupied throughout that period by the company or another person for agricultural purposes, and

o   the transferor owned them for a corresponding period of two years or seven years, as appropriate.

The relief extends to that part of the value of the shares or securities transferred by a chargeable transfer, which is attributable to the agricultural value of qualifying agricultural property. In some cases, the value of shares reduces under the rules that apply to the sale of related property within three years after death. Then the relief is only available if the shares sold were themselves sufficient to give the transferor control at the time of death.

Various points to note

- If the transferor inherits the property on a death, ownership, (and the period of occupation if it is subsequently occupied) runs from that date of death.
- If the transferor became entitled to the property on the death of a spouse or civil partner, relief is available for any period during which the spouse or civil partner owned or occupied it.
- Relief is available when the transferred property replaces other agricultural property.
- Occupation by a company that the transferor controls is treated as occupation by the transferor.
- If the transferred property was acquired on an earlier transfer, relief is available if;

o   the earlier transfer was eligible for relief
o   the earlier transfer was made to the current transferor or the transferor's spouse or civil partner

o the property at the time of the current transfer was occupied for agricultural purposes either by this transferor or by the personal representatives of the earlier transferor

o the property would qualify for relief apart from the occupation and ownership tests

o one of the transfers occurs on death.

Replacement property

If at the time of the second transfer the property replaces other property the relief is restricted to that which would have been available had the replacement not occurred.

A gift of agricultural property

The following rules relate to potentially exempt transfers which become chargeable, or where further tax becomes payable on an immediately chargeable transfer, as a result of the transferor's death within seven years of the transfer. Agricultural relief is available on property which qualified for relief at the time of the gift if that property-

- has been owned by the transferee throughout the period between the gift and the death of the transferor, or the earlier death of the transferee, and (subject to rules for replacement property) is not subject to a binding contract for sale, and

- is agricultural property immediately before the transferor's death, or the earlier death of the transferee, and has been occupied for agricultural purposes throughout the period between the gift and the death.

If the property that was originally given was shares in an agricultural company, the relief is only available if the original shares, or those treated by legislation as if they were original shares, have been retained through the relevant period. The agricultural property forming part of the company's assets must also have been:

- owned by the company, and
- occupied for agricultural purposes.

If only part of a gift qualifies for relief

If, at the date of the transferor's death the conditions for relief are satisfied for only part of the gifted property, a proportionate part of the value that was transferred is reduced.

If the transferee dies before the transferor the conditions for relief have to be satisfied at both the date of the gift and time of the transferee's death.

Rules for replacement property

Where the original agricultural property was disposed of before the transferor's death and the proceeds were used to buy replacement property, the relief is not necessarily lost.

In order to still qualify for relief:

- the whole of the sales proceeds must have been used to purchase the replacement property, and
- both the sale and purchase must have been at arm's length taking place within three years of each other.

Relief available if a gift of a farming business is replaced with other property

If the donee of a potentially exempt transfer (PET) of a farming business disposes of the business and replaces the business with a non-agricultural business, they will be denied agricultural relief on the value transferred by the PET. However, they can claim business relief if the conditions for that relief are satisfied.

Property replaced before a transfer by owner

This section deals with the relief available where property which would have qualified for the relief before the transfer, has been replaced by other property. The two year occupation condition is satisfied if the properties were occupied by the transferor, for the purposes of agriculture, for a total period of at least two years during the five years immediately before the transfer. The seven-year ownership test is satisfied if the properties were:

- owned by the transferor, and
- occupied (either personally or by another) for the purposes of agriculture for a total period of at least seven years during the ten years immediately before the transfer.

Business property replacing agricultural property

If business property replaces agricultural property which is part of a farming business, the period of ownership of the original property will be relevant for working out the original ownership condition to the replacement property.

Business relief will be available on the replacement if all the conditions for that relief are satisfied.

If a farming business is replaced by a non-agricultural business property, and the former is not eligible for agricultural relief, business relief may be claimed instead if the conditions for that relief are satisfied.

There are exceptions to this; for example, if agricultural land is not part of a farming business any replacement can only qualify for business property relief if it satisfies the minimum ownership conditions in its own right.

If the conditions for both agricultural relief and business relief are satisfied then agricultural relief is available instead of business relief. However, business relief may be available on a transfer of agricultural property which is not eligible for agricultural relief.

Woodland relief

IHT is potentially charged at 40% on the woodland of a deceased owner, though that only applies if the deceased person had assets of more than £325,000. There is also no IHT charged where assets are transferred to a spouse. This 40% tax is on the market value of the woodland so one can see that without various exemptions it would be hard to keep woodland in the family and hard to keep rural estates together. For woodland owners IHT can be legitimately avoided, reduced or deferred in three different ways.

The main way to avoid paying IHT is to make sure that the woodland qualifies as a business asset which formally means you would be using the Inheritance Tax Act of 1984 (IHTA) where you can get 100% relief from this tax if the woodland is both commercially managed (in other words it has been run as a business) and has been owned for at least 2 years. As the woodland owner you will need to show that the woodland has been managed with a view to generating timber income or capital gain from the increase in the value of the timber. The sorts of thing that HMRC look for are the existence of a management plan where the principal objective is timber production, evidence that the plan has been actioned and updated, and proof of budgets and financial records.

Usually, a Forestry-Commission-approved Woodland Management Plan will have been drawn up that also enables an owner to obtain grants which further help to prove "commerciality". Of course HMRC will look at the relief claim after death and it is up to the inheritor/beneficiary to provide the evidence on which HMRC can make a decision. However, it is quite possible that a woodland owner dies without having shown serious business intent, but all is not lost – there are two other routes to reduce or defer IHT.

The second route is the use of Agricultural Property Relief which essentially means that you can show that the woodland was part of an agricultural holding, perhaps used as a shelter belt. But this use has to be shown to be occupied along with agricultural land or pasture and also used in conjunction with it (ancillary use), so it is fairly unlikely that many owners of small woods – living some distance away from their woodlands – will be able to use this relief. However, there is a third IHT relief which many woodlands will be able to use, called "Woodland Relief". This allows IHT to be deferred on the value of the growing timber until such time as that timber is felled and sold, which in practice may be an almost indefinite period.

Quick succession relief

Quick succession relief is given when someone dies and his estate has been increased by a taxable disposition in his favour within the previous five years. The idea is to reduce the tax payable on the second transfer of assets within the five years. It is not essential for the property given by the first disposition to have been retained by the person concerned until the time of the second disposition.

The relief operates by reducing the tax payable on the second occasion by a sum equal to a percentage of the tax paid on the first occasion in respect of the increase in value of the second estate by the asset concerned. The increase is calculated on the basis of the net increase after deduction of tax and allowing for reliefs such as business relief but without any deduction for the expenses of administering the estate. It is a tax credit and it is the tax payable that is reduced, not the value of the asset. The percentage depends on how long has elapsed between the two dispositions:

- if less than one year has elapsed the percentage is 100%
- between one and two years 80%
- two and three years 60%
- between three and four years 40%
- between four and five years 20%

Relief for Heritage assets

Limited conditional relief is given in respect of land, buildings and objects which appear to the Treasury of being of outstanding importance from the point of view of national heritage. The relief is dependent on specified obligations to preserve the asset and allow public access to it being undertaken by the donor.

Death and military service

If a serving or former member of the Armed Forces dies from (or death can be shown to have been hastened by) an injury sustained or disease contracted on active service against the enemy or other service of a warlike nature (such as operations against hostile forces in peace time or anti-terrorist operations), a complete exemption from inheritance tax can be granted on their estate under the provisions of s154 of the Inheritance Tax Act. Likewise, whilst the total exemption is not transferable to a spouse's estate, the granting of an exemption on the veterans estate will double the personal tax threshold used to assess any Inheritance Tax liability on the spouses estate when they die.

Each application for an exemption is considered on its merits, after the death of the veteran concerned and requires the MoD to be given access to the veterans full medical records. Neither war time service in the armed forces, or receipt of a war pension, is a guarantee exemption will be granted. Anyone wishing to apply for an exemption under s154, on a veterans estate, or requiring further information, should contact

Veterans UK

Contact the agency, part of the Minsitry of Defence, for more information on service personnel on www.veterans-uk.info or on 0808 1914 2 18.

Relief for land and assets sold within a short time of death

It is sometimes possible to adjust for inheritance tax purposes the value attributed to any stock exchange securities (other than those quoted on the AIM market), shares in common investment funds, unit trusts, and land and buildings which are sold in the course of administration of the estate at a loss compared with their value as declared in the probate papers, to reflect the sale price rather than the value at the date of death.

To obtain an agreement by HMRC to a revaluation in the case of stock exchange securities, shares in common investment funds and unit trusts they must have been sold within twelve months of the date of the death.

Deeds of Family Arrangement

It is possible for the beneficiaries of a will, or those who inherit a share of an estate upon intestacy, to vary the terms of the will or the inheritance on intestacy by agreement after the death. This is done by a voluntary agreement contained in a document known as a Deed of family Arrangement or by a deed of disclaimer. Similarly, the personal representatives of a beneficiary who survives his benefactor and then dies can vary the inheritance if they have the consent of those who benefit under his will or upon his intestacy If this special provision was not made then any such variation would constitute a taxable disposition. Basically, under the Inheritance Tax Act if a variation is made within two years of the death and certain other conditions are complied with, the transfer shall not be considered a transfer of value and the variation is viewed as if it had been made by the deceased. Distributions made within two years of the testator's death from discretionary trusts created by his will are also considered to have been made by the deceased's will.

Double taxation relief

If an asset which is situated overseas is subject to a tax similar to inheritance tax in a foreign country and also to inheritance tax in the UK, relief will be given as a credit against UK tax payable in respect of the overseas asset. The relief given is the lower of the foreign tax which has been paid in respect of the asset and the UK tax which would otherwise be payable in respect of the asset, the UK tax being calculated at the average percentage rate payable in respect of the estate.

Limiting the set-off of debts

Following the introduction of the Finance Act 2013, new rules were brought into play concerning set-off of debts. Where a non-domiciled individual (or the trustees of his trust) borrow from a bank secured on a UK property and deposit the borrowed funds on a back to back basis (or use them for investing offshore) the debt will not be allowable on the individual's death. This will increase the inheritance taxable estate. Nor will the debt be allowable in calculating inheritance tax charges in the trust.

Entrepreneurs who borrow to invest in their business but secure the borrowing on other assets will have the borrowing deducted from the business assets leaving their family with a bigger inheritance tax bill. This also applies where the borrowings are used in relation to agricultural property and woodlands. Debts which are not repaid after an individual's death, may also be disallowed. The time limit for repayment is not specified but the debt must be discharged "after death, out of the estate" which suggests that it must be repaid in the course of administration of the estate if it is to be allowable. Debts are not disallowed where there is a "real commercial reason" for the debt not being repaid. This will be the case where there is an arm's length borrowing or, if the borrowing is from someone other than a third party, a third party in the same circumstances would not require the debt to be paid.

In addition the liability must not be left unpaid as part of "arrangements where the main purpose, or one of the main purposes, is to secure a tax advantage".

The definitions of "arrangements" and "tax advantage" are very wide. A tax advantage includes a delay in a charge to tax or even the avoidance of a possible assessment or determination in respect of tax as well as obtaining a relief or repayment or reduction in the tax. "Tax" is expressly defined to include income tax and capital gains tax.

Before the disguised remuneration provisions were introduced, it was common for Employee Benefit Trusts (EBTs) to make loans to beneficiaries which were left outstanding indefinitely and might be waived after the individual's death. These sorts of loans will, if not repaid by the estate after the ex-employee's death, be disallowed in calculating inheritance tax. This creates a catch-22 situation. The disguised remuneration rules provide that if the loan is waived after death, the individual's estate or heirs will be subject to an income tax charge. But if the loan remains outstanding, there is no deduction from the estate, potentially increasing the inheritance tax due.

Chapter 6

Trusts

In this chapter we will cover the following:

- Definition of a trust
- Property
- Beneficiaries
- Creation of a trust
- Trustees
- Different types of trusts
- Taxation of trusts
- Trusts and capital gains tax

Trusts can be a very effective tool indeed when planning inheritance tax and it is essential to know the basics of trusts and how they can be utilised.

Definition of a trust

Put simply, a trust is an obligation binding a person, or persons, which can be an individual or company, (a trust can have up to four trustees) to deal with 'property' in a particular way, for the benefit of one or more beneficiaries.

Trustees

Trustees are the legal owners of the trust property. They are legally bound to look after the property of the trust in a particular way and for a particular purpose. Trustees administer the trust and in certain circumstances make decisions about how the property in the trust is to be used. Trustees can change, but there must be a minimum of one trustee.

Property

The property of a trust can include:

- Money
- Investments
- Land or buildings
- Other assets

The cash and investments held in a trust are also called the 'capital' or 'fund' of the trust. The capital or fund may produce income and the land or buildings may produce income. The way income is taxed will depend on the nature or type of the trust.

The beneficiary of the trust

A beneficiary is anyone who benefits from the property held in the trust. There can be any number of beneficiaries, such as a whole family or class of people and each can benefit from the trust in a different way. Beneficiaries can benefit from:

- Income only
- Capital only
- Both the income and capital

The Settlor

A settler is anyone who has put property into a trust. The trust may be created by an express statement of the settlor (an express trust) or by implication from his conduct or presumed intention (an implied or resulting trust) or imposed by law to achieve fairness in a certain situation (constructive trust). This section is concerned with express trusts. Property is normally put into a trust when it is created but it can be added at a later time.

Creating a trust

Normally, a trust is created by deed. Usually, a settlor will ask a professional advisor to draw up a trust deed, which in turn sets out the terms of the trust. A trust can be created under the terms of a will, when someone leaves instructions that when he or she dies all or some of the estate is placed in trust. A trust can also occur if someone dies without leaving a will Sometimes a court will create a trust, for example when deciding how to deal with property for the benefit of children or for someone who is incapacitated in some way.

The responsibilities of a trustee

The trustee will have to make provision for any tax owed. The responsibility of a trustee will depend very much on the type of trust (see below for explanation of the different trusts). The settlor may have given instructions that trustees carry out certain functions and the law may impose other duties. For tax purposes the trustee is responsible for:

- Notifying the HMRC that income tax is due, within six months of the end of the tax year for which it is due
- Keeping records of the income and capital gains of the trust
- Completing and sending back tax returns relating to the trust
- Paying any tax due

- Supplying certificates or vouchers to the beneficiaries to show how much income they have received from the trust in the tax year and how much tax the trustees have deducted. Professional advisors may be appointed but it is ultimately the trustees responsibility.

As a trustee, if a trust is wound up HMRC should be notified and final tax returns completed. Provisions will have to be made for any tax owed.

The different sorts of trust

Although there are a number of different sorts of trust they will usually fall into one of the below categories:

- Bare trusts
- Interest in possession trusts
- Discretionary trusts
- Accumulation and maintenance trusts
- Mixed trusts

For tax purposes, there are also settlor-interested trusts and non-resident trusts and special trusts.

The bare trust

A bare trust, also known as a simple trust, is one in which each beneficiary has an immediate and absolute right to both capital and income. The beneficiaries of a bare trust have the right to take actual possession of trust property.

The (limited) interest in possession trust

This type of trust exists when a beneficiary, known in this case as an 'income beneficiary' has a current legal right to the income from the trust as it arises. The trustees must pass over all the income received, less any trustees expenses and taxes, to the beneficiary.

A beneficiary who is entitled to the income of the trust for life is known as a life tenant, or as having a life interest. The income beneficiary need not, and often does not, have any rights over the capital of such a trust. Normally, the capital will pass over to a different beneficiary(s) at a specific time in the future or after a specific event. Depending o the terms of the trust, the trustees might have the power to pay capital to a beneficiary even though the beneficiary only has the right to receive income. A beneficiary who is entitled to the trust capital is known as the 'remainderman', or the 'capital beneficiary'.

Uses for interest in possession trusts

Interest in possession trusts are very useful in the case of second or subsequent marriages if a taxpayer wishes his assets to benefit his spouse after his death but to ensure that they are inherited by his/her children and no one else after his/her death.

Interest in possession trusts are also useful to provide for the maintenance of individual children in a family until they are capable of providing for themselves.

The discretionary trust

Trustees of a discretionary trust generally have discretion about how to use the income of the trust. They may be required to use the income for the benefit f any specific beneficiaries, but can also decide:

- How much is paid

- To which beneficiary or class of beneficiaries payments are made
- How often payments are made
- What (if any) conditions to impose on the beneficiaries

The trustees may, or may not, be allowed to 'accumulate' income within the trust for as long as the law allows rather than pass it to the beneficiaries. Income that has been accumulated becomes part of the assets of the trust.

Age 18 to 25 trust

From 22 March 2006, an `age 18 to 25 trust' is a discretionary trust set up under the will or intestacy of a deceased parent or step-parent, where the property is held on trust for the benefit of someone aged over 18 and under 25. Accumulation and maintenance trusts set up before 22 March 2006 which provide for the beneficiaries to become absolutely entitled to the trust fund on or before the age of 25 will become age 18 to 25 trust if, before 6 April 2008, they rewrite the trust to comply with the new rules. The property in an 18 to 25 trust is subject to age18 to 25 exit charges when property leaves the trust on or before the beneficiary's twenty-fifth birthday.

Uses of discretionary trusts

The principal advantage of a discretionary trust is that no inheritance tax is payable upon the death of a potential beneficiary because no beneficiary has a right to a defined interest in the trust assets or the income that they produce until the trustees have exercised their discretion in his favour. A further benefit is that of flexibility. Within the wide boundaries set out in a trust deed a discretionary trust permits the trustees to use the trust fund in any way that they consider to be most appropriate at the time. Discretionary trusts are frequently used to provide for people whose financial needs are likely to vary at different times in the future or to protect the trust fund from creditors if one of the potential beneficiaries is a spendthrift or engaged in risky business ventures that could end in bankruptcy.

Trust for disabled people

A discretionary trust set up for the benefit of a disabled person. After 9 March 1991 these trust were treated as if the disabled person had an interest in possession in the property held in the trust. Any distributions from the trust to the disabled person are not taxable, but a charge to IHT will arise on their death and the trust fund will form part of their estate.

Accumulation and maintenance trust

Up to 22 March 2006, an accumulation and maintenance trust (A&M trust) was a discretionary trust where the property in the trust was held for the maintenance, education or benefit of the beneficiaries or accumulated until the beneficiaries reach the age of 25. The property in these trusts was not subject to proportionate charges (ten-yearly-charges). From 22 March 2006, if the trustees changed the terms of the trust before 6 April 2008 to ensure that the beneficiary becomes absolutely entitled to the property in the trust on or before their 18th birthday, the trust will continue to be an A&M trust. If the trustees changed the terms before 6 April 2008 to ensure that the beneficiary becomes absolutely entitled to the property in the trust between their 18th and 25th birthdays, the trust will become an age 18 to 25 trust and is the subject to an age

18 to 25 exit charge whenever property leaves the trust and on the 25th birthday of the beneficiary. If nothing was done to change the terms of existing A&M trusts before 6 April 2008, they would have become relevant property trusts and will be subject to proportionate charges.

Mixed trust

A mixed trust is a mixture of more than one type of trust, for example:

- An interest in possession trust and a discretionary trust, or
- An interest in possession trust and an accumulation and maintenance trust

Settlor-interested trust

There are special tax rules in which the settlor 'retains an interest' in the trust for example where the settlor receives an income from the trust. However, this type of trust will not be covered further because of its highly specialised nature.

Non-resident trusts and special trusts

Again the rules for these trusts are too complicated and would need a professional advisor to elaborate these rules. Examples of such trusts include:

- Trusts where some or all of the trustees are not UK residents
- Trusts that are not created or are not administered under UK law

- Various special types of UK trust such as charities, pension funds, unit trusts and trusts for employee share schemes.

The taxation of trusts

The tax regime covers the different types of trusts in relation to capital gains tax, income tax and also inheritance tax. In the first section we deal with income tax and capital gains tax and then finally inheritance tax. Depending on the type of trust, when income and capital gains tax arise in a trust, tax might be charged on:

- The trustees
- The beneficiaries
- The settlor

Taxation of trusts generally

A trust, for UK tax purposes, is a separate legal entity and the trustees of a trust are considered as a body distinct from the individuals who compose it.

Taxation of trusts must be considered in respect of inheritance tax, capital gains tax and income tax at three stages of its existence: when assets are transferred into the trust, during the continuance of the trust and when assets are transferred out of the trust, including when the trust terminates.

Taxation of bare trusts

Bare trusts are created for tax purposes as if the beneficiary holds the trust property in his or her own name. Income tax and capital gains tax are charged on the beneficiary. The beneficiary must declare any income and capital gains on their personal tax return. Although trustees can pay income tax on behalf of a beneficiary, it is the beneficiary who is chargeable to tax.

Interest in possession trusts and tax

The trustees of this type of trust are normally chargeable to income tax on income received.

- rent and trading income are chargeable at the basic rate (currently 20% (2017-18)
- UK dividend income is chargeable at the starting rate for dividends (currently 7.5%) and the tax credit attached to the net dividend meets the trustee's liability
- Savings income, such as bank interest, is chargeable on the trustees at the lower rate (20%). Such income usually has tax deducted at source by the bank or the building society and this is taken into account in taxing the trustees.

The beneficiaries are entitled to the income from the trust after tax and expenses, and are taxed on this in the normal way. They are entitled to credit for tax paid by the trustees or deducted at source. If beneficiaries are starting rate taxpayers or non-taxpayers they will be able to claim some or all of the tax paid, though tax credits on dividends cannot be claimed. If they are liable at higher rates then further tax will be due.

Accumulation and Discretionary trusts and tax

Trustees are responsible for declaring and paying Income Tax on income received by the trust. They do this on form SA900 Trust and Estate Tax Return each year.

In both discretionary trusts and accumulation trusts, income is taxed at the special trust rates, apart from the first £1,000 of trust income, which is known as the 'standard rate band'. Income that falls within the standard rate band is taxed at lower rates, depending on the nature of the income - as shown in the tables below.

However, if the person who put the assets into the trust (the settlor) has more than one trust, the £1,000 standard rate band is divided by the number of trusts they have. If the settlor has more than five trusts, the standard rate band is £200 for each trust.

Trust income up to £1000

Type of income	Tax rate 2017-18 tax year
Rent, trading and savings	20% (basic rate)
UK dividends such as income from stocks and shares	7.5% (dividend ordinary rate)

Trust income over £1000

Type of income	Tax rate 2017-18 tax year
Dividends and distributions	38.1% (dividend trust rate)
Other income	45% (trust rate)

Mixed trusts

Mixed trusts will be taxed under the rules for that type of trust, e.g. the part of a trust that is an interest in possession will be taxed as such and so on.

Payment of tax

Trustees may need to pay tax for any one year in three instalments, as follows:

- a payment on account on 31st January in the tax year
- another payment on account on 31st July after the end of the tax year, and
- a final payment on the following 31st January, if further tax is due.

Trusts and capital gains tax

Capital gains tax is charged when an asset that is not exempt from the tax is disposed of. Capital gains tax is charged upon any increase in the value of the asset (the gain) between the date of its acquisition and its disposal.

From the capital gain can be deducted the cost of acquiring the asset, increasing its value, defending one's title to and disposing of the asset. Assets which are exempt from capital gains tax are:

- UK government stock
- Savings certificates
- Premium bonds
- Assets held in peps
- Assets held in ISA's

- Cash held in sterling
- Foreign currency held for personal use
- Chattels valued at £6,000 or less
- Private motor cars
- The taxpayer's principal private residence with land in total not exceeding one half a hectare.
- Betting, lottery or polls winnings

Capital gains tax on death

No capital gains tax is payable by a deceased person's personal representatives at the time of the death on the assets of the estate and for the purpose of capital gains tax the personal representatives are deemed to acquire the assets at their probate valuation.

Trusts (other than bare trusts and settlor interested trusts) are treated as separate entities for the purpose of capital gains tax and transfers into and out of trusts are treated as disposals. In the case of a bare trust, the assets of the trust are considered to be those of the beneficiary. In the case of a settlor interested trust any capital gains liability of the trust is considered to be that of the settlor.

****

Chapter 7

Payment of Inheritance Tax

In this chapter we will cover the following:

- Responsibility for payment of inheritance tax
- Payment in instalments

Either the person responsible for payment of tax (primary person) or the recipient of the gift (secondary person) will be responsible for inheritance tax. If HMRC cannot or choose not to obtain payment from the primary person then they will charge the secondary person. Taxation of inheritance tax is a pyramid responsibility. On death, all the inheritance tax due in respect of an asset can be recovered from anyone entitled to an interest in the asset as a result of death. If the secondary person pays the tax, or a person with no interest in the asset pays it, this tax can be recovered from the person further up the ladder.

Inheritance tax payable on an immediately chargeable transfer will be paid by the donor unless agreed otherwise between donor and donee. If borne by the donor the gift must be 'grossed up', which means that the gift is considered to be the sum given and the amount of the tax payable because that is the amount by which the donor's estate is diminished.

Additional tax may be due on immediately chargeable gifts and potentially exempt transfers when the donor dies within seven years. If the person making the immediately chargeable gift dies within seven years then the responsibility for payment of IHT is that of the donee, or the person who receives the benefit of the gift. Any additional tax payable on a PET because of the death of the donor within seven years of making the gift is primarily the responsibility of the person to whom the gift is given or who receives a benefit from it. In the above cases, if the tax is not paid within 12 months of death, HMRC can also recover it from the deceased's representatives out of the estate.

Trust funds

If the trustees of a trust make a transfer of value, any tax owed will be the responsibility of the trustees to be paid out of the funds held in trust. However, if a transfer of value is the result of the death of a disabled person entitled to the income of a trust for the disabled for the rest of his life, the tax payable on death is borne by the deceased's personal representatives in proportion to the relative values of the deceased's own estate and the trust fund.

Residuary estates

If a persons will leaves the residuary estate to exempt beneficiaries and to taxable beneficiaries, any inheritance tax payable must be paid out of the shares of the taxable beneficiaries after the estate has been divided but before distribution.

Other bequests

The wording of a will can determine who bears any inheritance tax on bequests made by the will. Unless otherwise stated in the will, tax is borne by those who inherit the residuary estate. The one exception is that of foreign or jointly owned property in which case the tax is payable by the beneficiary of the property.

When is IHT due?

In the case of an immediately chargeable gift made between 6th April and 30th September, the inheritance tax is due on the 30th April of the following year. Tax on immediately chargeable gifts made between 1st October and 5th April is payable by six months after the end of the month in which a gift is made. If any additional tax becomes payable in respect of an immediately chargeable gift or inheritance tax is payable as a result of a donor of a potentially exempt transfer dying within seven years of making the gift, tax is payable six months after the end of the month in which the donor dies.

Tax can be paid in instalments on the below assets, ten equal annual instalments, if the transfer occurs on death, the first instalment being payable six months after the end of the month in which the person died:

- land and buildings
- timber
- net value of a business or an interest in a business
- Controlling shareholdings in a company
- Holdings of unquoted shares whose minimum value is at least £20,000 and which represent at least 10% of the company's issued share capital, or if they are ordinary shares, 10% of the company's issued ordinary share capital

- Holdings of unquoted shares in respect of which the tax could not be paid without undue hardship
- Holdings of unquoted shares, if the tax on them and other assets for which payment by instalments is permissible exceeds 20% of the tax payable by one person in the same capacity.

If the tax is payable by the donee in respect of a PET of the above categories of assets, there may be an option to pay by instalments, but only if the assets are still owned by the donee at the date of the donor's death.

When the asset is sold, or an asset ceases to be held by a trust the option to pay by instalments ceases.

****

Chapter 8

Inheritance Tax-Reducing the bill

In this chapter we will cover the following:
- Gifts and exemptions
- Gifts with reservation of benefits
- Life assurance
- The family home
- Wills and deeds of variation
- Charity

As we have seen throughout the book, there are various ways of handling inheritance tax in order to reduce the actual burden on beneficiaries and executors of the estate. This chapter draws the various strands together and reminds you what can be done during your lifetime to reduce your inheritance tax bill.

As we have also seen, those above the nil-rate band of inheritance tax, currently £325,000 in 2017/2018 will be liable to pay 40% of the value of the estate above the band. We need to refresh ourselves on what can be done to ensure that the actual value of the estate is kept to a minimum. First, we should look at gifts and exemptions.

Gifts and exemptions

Generally speaking, gifts made during a person's lifetime are not chargeable to IHT when made but constitute a Potentially Exempt Transfer. Unless you have reserved a benefit in the asset concerned, these gifts are not treated as taxable for inheritance tax purposes as long as you survive for a period of seven years after making the gift. If you do not survive then the gift is added to the value of the estate upon your death. Taking this into account, it is therefore wise to consider giving away as much as you can. As far as larger gifts are concerned, it is also wise to consider whether or not the beneficiary is mature enough to cope with the size of the gift or whether it is prudent to put the gift into a trust, as described in the previous chapters.

The nil-rate band also operates in respect of lifetime gifts, with these being accounted for on a rolling seven-year basis. Should a gift become chargeable to IHT, either because it has been made during lifetime to a company or to a trust and the nil-rate band has been exceeded, or because you die within seven years, there are a number of relief's and exemptions that apply. The most important of these is gifts in full to a UK domiciled spouse or to a registered civil partner. There are exemptions for gifts out of disposable income, gifts to political parties, charities and for national purposes. dispositions for the maintenance of family, small gifts of less than £250 per person per tax year and gifts in the occasion of the recipient's marriage. There is also an annual exemption of £3,000 per tax year which, if unused, can be carried forward to the next year (for one year only). It is therefore very important to have a firm grasp of gifts and exemptions in order to ensure that adequate planning takes place during your own lifetime.

Gifts with reservation of benefit and the pre-owned assets tax
A gift where you have reserved a right to benefit from the asset, for example, continued occupation of your house) may well be

ineffective for the purposes of IHT. If there is to be no clean break it is vital that you take appropriate advice. The existence of a number of schemes designed to get round the gifts with reservation of benefit rules led to the introduction of the 'pre-owned assets tax'. This pre-owned assets tax must be taken into account in any future planning.

Life assurance

Making contributions to a life policy is a very useful planning tool when considering future IHT liability, involving gifts. Policies are typically written in trust so that the proceeds do not form part of the policy holder's estate on death. This means that they can be used to provide for an IHT liability, either in respect of the full estate (whole of life policies) or in the case of death within seven years of making a gift (term assurance) without adding to the sum chargeable. The changes to the IHT trust regime introduced by the Finance Act 2006, however, can impact upon life policies and advice should be taken when large sums are involved.

There is also a wide range of investment products linked to life cover that form part of the IHT planning toolbox and that can again provide for a solution in the right circumstances. Again, more specialist advice should be taken in this area.

The family home

The family home represents probably the most sizeable chunk of most people's assets and will form the bulk of the estate. It is important that you have knowledge of the ways to treat the family home in respect of IHT.

When a property is owned by more than one person (for example husband and wife) that ownership can take one of two forms. A joint tenancy will mean that the property will pass automatically to the survivor on the death of a joint owner. A tenancy in common means that the share of each owner will pass according to the terms of their will (or if appropriate the rules of intestacy) A tenancy in common permits for more flexibility in dealing with the family home and for this reason a change in ownership might well be considered wise for IHT planning.

Gifting your home to your children

You may want to gift your home to a child. However, if you do this you should bear in mind that:

- gifts to your children-unlike gifts to your spouse or to your civil partner-aren't exempt from inheritance tax unless you live for seven years after making them
- if you keep living there without paying a full market rent it is not an 'outright gift' but a gift with reservation so its still treated as part of your estate and liable for IHT
- from 6th April 2005, you may be liable to pay an income tax charge on the benefit you get from having free or low cost use of the property you formerly owned or provided funds to purchase
- Once you have given your home away your children own it and it becomes part of their assets, so if they are bankrupted or divorced the home may have to be sold to pay creditors or as part of a divorce settlement

- If your children sell your home, and it is not their main home, they will have to pay capital gains tax on any increase in value.

Downsizing to a smaller property

If you decide to downsize to a smaller property and give away the proceeds of the sale of the larger property, these gifts may qualify as:

- Potentially exempt transfers so they wouldn't be taxable unless you die within seven years
- Part of your annual exemption in £3000 chunks each year.

Given that your property probably forms the bulk of your estate it is essential that you know what you are going to do with it before HMRC takes a large slice of the value on death.

Wills and deeds of variation

One of the most important aspects of IHT planning is that of ensuring that you have a valid will in place. If you die without making a will your estate will be divided among family members according to the laws of intestacy. See chapter ten. Not only might this run totally counter to your wishes but it can also be very inefficient in terms of IHT planning. Have a will drawn up professionally, take expert advice. The costs are small compared with what might be at stake. Ensure that your will is subject to regular review. You should keep in mind that your will may cease to be valid if you marry or remarry.

If you die intestate or with a poorly devised will it is currently possible for relevant beneficiaries to enter into a deed of variation that, subject to time limits, can have the effect of putting things right for the purposes of IHT. A deed of variation is a document that alters a will posthumously and can be used to limit tax liability. It can be made at any time within two years of the death of the person who made the will and it's purpose is to reduce IHT or capital gains tax, move assets into a trust, add a beneficiary who has been left out of a will or to correct an error. They are effective retrospectively from the time of death and any amendments are treated as though they are made by the deceased.

Wills Trusts and the equalisation of estates

Probably the most common IHT planning technique is the drafting of husband and wife wills to include a clause (typically establishing a Will Trust) that ensures that full use is made of the nil-rate band. If, on the first death, everything passes to a UK domiciled spouse there will be no IHT charge: however, on the second death the whole of the estate will be charged IHT. If, however, the first to die leaves a sum equivalent to the available nil-rate band to other beneficiaries there will still be no IHT payable and the joint estate is reduced by that sum.

Overall, therefore, both husband and wife will benefit from two nil-rate bands rather than just one-with a tax saving. However, planning of this sort must be accompanied by steps to ensure that the estates of husband and wife are equivalent to the extent that both include free assets at least to the value of the nil-rate band.

Deathbed planning

It should not be assumed that nothing can be done to plan or reduce IHT just because a person is elderly. Given the long life span, gifts in the hope of surviving seven years should not be ruled out. Sizeable gifts will benefit from the tapering of the associated IHT charge where the individual survives for more than three years. If survival for two years is a reasonable prospect, it may be considering a switch to investments that will enjoy business or agricultural property relief at the end of that period. Shares quoted on the Alternative Investment market (AIM) are an obvious option, with an increasing number of packaged products available. Even for those whose expectancy is measured in months rather than years it is important to review the position and ensure that there are no obstacles to obtaining relief. In limited circumstances there may be scope to change the status of assets to secure business or agricultural relief. Consideration should also be given to a number of investment base products that can achieve an IHT saving in this sort of situation

Charity

Finally, if you intend to give the bulk of your estate to charity, it may be the case that you can forget about IHT. Do bear in mind however the other tax relief's that are available for lifetime charitable giving and the possibility that these may be used to boost your charitable giving further. In particular the creation of a charitable trust or foundation during lifetime may be an attractive proposition if you wish to donate considerable sums.

New rules affecting pensions

From April 2015, if a person dies before the age of 75 they can pass funds left in their pension to beneficiaries completely free of tax and no tax will be paid on the money that they withdraw from that pension. Previously, a punitive 55% was charged If a person dies after the age of 75 their beneficiaries will be able to draw on income from the pension pot, charged at their marginal rate (highest rate) of income, 20-40 or 45%. Alternatively, if they take the money as a lump sum they will be taxed at 45%. For more information on both private and state pensions and inheritance tax go to www.gov.uk/tax-on-pension-death-benefits

****

Chapter 9

Valuing an Estate and Applying for Probate

In this chapter we will look at the following:

- When to value an estate
- Assets of an estate
- Debts and liabilities
- Probate

This book is about inheritance tax, therefore one of the most important elements is that of the valuation of a person's estate, in order to ensure that you have an accurate idea of its worth and also of your inheritance tax liability. This topic was covered in the first few chapters but it is worth reiterating again within the context of the process of obtaining probate.

When valuing a deceased person's estate you must include property, possessions and money they owned at the time of their death, as well as certain gifts they may have made up to seven years before they died. Your valuation must reflect the current market value of the assets.

When you have to value an estate
Valuing the estate of someone who has died is one of the first things to do if you are acting as the executor or personal representative for the estate. You normally can't get access to the assets in the estate

until you have received a grant of probate (or confirmation in Scotland). You need to know the estates worth to fill in the probate application form and show whether or not inheritance tax is due.

Assets of an estate

The assets of an estate are anything that has value, such as:

- money in accounts, building society, banks or other
- businesses or business assets owned by the deceased or a business partnership of which they were a member
- houses and land including farmland
- Stocks and shares
- Personal belongings such as antiques or jewellery
- Furniture and other fixtures in houses
- Motor vehicles
- Pensions that include a lump sum payment on death
- Assets in a trust from which the deceased benefited
- Life insurance payouts
- Other assets held abroad

The following should be evaluated to see if they are exempt:

- any assets given away in the seven years before death
- any asset that the deceased gave away at any time, but in which they retained an interest
- any assets jointly owned with someone else

Debts and liabilities

Debts and liabilities have to be balanced against assets. Liabilities include expenses from administering the estate. Examples include:

- mortgages outstanding
- debts on credit cards
- overdrafts
- unpaid taxes
- household bills
- outstanding loans
- funeral expenses

There are then a number of steps to take in arriving at the value of the estate.

a) Work out the market value of the assets and gifts

Finding out the market value of assets can be simple in some cases and more complicated in others. For example you may need to use a surveyor to value property. You need to remember to include any gifts (money, property or assets) that the deceased gave away that were not exempt. If you don't know the exact value of any item and the value of the estate is likely to be less than £200,000 then an accurate estimated figure will do. Once you have completed this exercise you then add together the value of all the assets.

b) Deduct any debts

Deduct from the total market value of the assets anything that the deceased or the estate owed.

c) Make a record of the valuation

The value of all the assets minus all the debts is the value of the estate. These should be listed and a record kept of all the paperwork involved in the valuations should also be kept.

d) Decide if any heritance tax is due and which forms should be used. You will need different forms depending on where the deceased lived and whether inheritance tax is due. For a list of all the appropriate forms you should go to HMRC website (address at back of the book which lists all the appropriate forms.

Inheritance tax and the probate process

Probate (or confirmation in Scotland) is the system you go through if you are handling the estate of someone who has died. It gives you the legal right to distribute the estate according to the deceased's wishes. Inheritance tax forms are part of the process even if the estate doesn't owe inheritance tax.

Probate terminology

If the deceased left a will, it will usually name one or more 'executors' who apply for grant of probate (also called a grant of representation).

If the deceased died without leaving a will, a blood relative can apply for a 'grant of letters of administration' depending on a strict next-of-kin order of priority defined in the rules of intestacy. This makes that person the administrator.

If the named executor doesn't want to act, someone else named in the will can apply to be the administrator (again depending on a strict order of priority).

Scotland and Ireland have their own terms, having different legal systems. The terminology is generally the same in Northern Ireland. However, in Scotland the process is called confirmation, and the personal representative applies for a grant of representation. Different forms are utilised in Scotland and Northern Ireland. The Northern Ireland Court Service website gives useful information on probate and other areas.

The process of probate

In England and Wales, the process is as follows:

- Value the estate as above and speak to the banks and other financial institutions to see whether you need probate
- If you need probate, complete the relevant probate and inheritance application forms-these differ depending on whether or not the estate owes inheritance tax
- Send the forms to the relevant government bodies. In England and Wales that's the controlling Probate Registry and HM Revenue and Customs (HMRC)
- Pay whatever inheritance tax is due
- Attend an interview at the Probate Registry and swear an oath
- Wait for the grant of probate to arrive in the post
- Pay any debts owed by the estate and then distribute the estate

Probate may not be needed if the estate:

- is a low-value estate-generally worth less than £5,000 and doesn't include land property or shares. In other words is low value and uncomplicated
- passes to the surviving spouse/civil partner because it was held in joint names.

You will almost certainly need probate if the estate includes:

- assets worth more than £5,000
- land or property in the name of the deceased, or held as tenants in common with someone else
- stocks or shares
- some insurance policies.

When applying for probate you will need to fill out an inheritance tax form in addition to the PA1 Probate Application form, even if the estate doesn't owe inheritance tax. The estate will only owe tax if it is over the threshold (£325,000 2017/18).

For more details on valuing an estate you should go to www.gov.uk/valuing-estate-of-someone-who-died/assets

****

Chapter 10

Wills Generally and Inheritance Tax

In this chapter we will cover the following:

- Making a will
- Inheritance issues
- Inheritance tax and your will

It is easy to put off making a will. If you die without one your assets may be distributed according to the law as opposed to your wishes. This could mean that your partner receives less or family members get a share, contrary to your own preferences.

Making a will-why its important

There are lots of good financial reasons for making a will:

- you can decide how your assets are shared out
- if you aren't married or in a civil partnership your partner will not inherit automatically-you can make sure that your partner is provided for
- if you are divorced or your civil partnership has been dissolved you can decide whether to leave anything to an ex-partner who is living with someone else
- you can make sure that you don't pay more inheritance tax than is necessary

Who inherits if you don't have a will?

If you don't have a will there are rules for deciding who inherits your assets, depending on your circumstances. The following rules are for deaths after February 1ˢᵗ 2009 in England and Wales.

The law differs if you die without a will in Scotland and Northern Ireland. The rates that applied before that date are shown in brackets.

If you are married or in a civil partnership without children

The husband, wife or civil partner won't automatically get everything although they will receive:

- personal items, such as household articles and cars, but nothing used for business purposes
- £400,000 (£200,000) free of tax-or the whole estate if it was less than £400,000
- half of the rest of the estate

The other half of the rest of the estate will be shared by the following:

- surviving parents
- if there are no surviving parents, any brothers and sisters (who shared the same two parents as the deceased) will get a share (or their children if they died while the deceased was still alive
- if the deceased has none of the above, the husband, wife, or registered civil partner will get everything.

If married or in a civil partnership with children

Your husband, wife or civil partner won't automatically get everything, although they will receive:

- personal items, such as household articles and cars but nothing used for business purposes
- £250,000 (£125,000) tax free or the whole of the estate if worth less than £250,000
- a life interest in half of the rest of the estate (on his or her death this will pass to the children)
- the rest of the estate will be shared by the children.

If you are partners but are not married or in a civil partnership

If you aren't married or registered civil partners, you won't automatically get a share of your partner's estate if they die without making a will. If they haven't provided for you in some other way, your only option is to make a claim under the Inheritance (Provision for Family and Dependents) Act 1975. To make a claim you must have a particular type of relationship with the deceased, such as child, spouse, civil partner, dependant or cohabite. You need to make a claim within six months of the grant of letters of administration. You will almost certainly need legal advice if pursuing such a claim.

If there is no surviving spouse or civil partner

The estate is distributed as follows (overleaf):

- to surviving children in equal shares (or to their children if they died whilst the deceased was still alive
- if there are no children, to parents (equally if both alive)

- if there are no surviving parents, to brothers and sisters (who shared the same two parents as the deceased) or to their children if they died while the deceased was still alive
- if there are no brothers or sisters then to half brothers or sisters (or to their children if they died while the deceased was still alive
- if none of the above then to grandparents (equally if more than one)
- if there are no grandparents then to aunts and uncles (or their children if they died while the deceased was still alive)
- if none of the above then to half uncles and aunts (or their children if they died while the deceased was still alive)
- to the Crown if there are none of the above.

Inheritance tax and your will

If you leave everything to your husband, wife or civil partner

In this case there will usually not be any inheritance tax to pay because, as we have seen, a husband, wife or civil partner counts as an exempt beneficiary. However, if you are domiciled in the UK but your spouse or civil partner isn't, you can only leave them £55,000 tax free. You should check this figure with HMRC as like everything it is subject to change.

Other beneficiaries

You can leave up to £325,000 tax-free to anyone in your will, not just your spouse or civil partner. So you could, for example, give some of your estate to someone else or a family trust. IHT is then payable at 40% on any amount you leave above this.

****

Useful addresses and websites

Inheritance tax

www.direct.gov.uk

This is the official government website with a complete breakdown of inheritance tax

HM Revenue and Customs (HMRC)

www.gov.uk/government/organisations/hm-revenue-customs

This is the website of Her Majesty's Revenue and Customs with a complete breakdown of all allowances.

Probate

www.justice.gov.uk/courts/probate

Gives guidance on all matters concerned with probate

London Probate Department
PRFD
First Avenue
42-49 High Holborn
Ground Floor
Holborn
London WC1V 6NP
Tel: 0207 421 8509

Citizens Advice Bureau

https://www.citizensadvice.org.uk

Gives advice on all matters to do with Inheritance Tax

WHICH

www.which.co.uk/money/tax/inheritance-tax

Has very useful advice pages relating to Inheritance tax generally.

****

Inheritance Tax: Glossary of terms

Accumulation
When the income of the fund is saved up and not paid out to any beneficiaries, it is said to be accumulated.

Administrator
A man who is appointed by the courts to administer a deceased person's estate in England, Wales and Northern Ireland; usually where there is no will or they are not named in the will.

Administratrix
A woman who is appointed by the courts to administer a deceased person's estate in England, Wales and Northern Ireland; usually where there is no will or they are not named in the will.

Agricultural relief
Relief from Inheritance tax that is due on the transfer of agricultural property. The relief applies to the agricultural value of the asset only.

Agricultural property.
Land or pasture used in the growing of crops or rearing of animals for food consumption, also can include farmhouses and farm cottages.

Agricultural value
The value a property would have if it could only be used as agricultural property. More on agricultural value.

Annual exemption

The amount you can give away each tax year that will be exempt from Inheritance tax . This is currently £3,000 and applies to one gift or a number of gifts up to that amount. There are other exemptions which can apply.

Annuity

A series of fixed payments paid over a fixed number of years or during the lifetime of an individual, or both. An annuity is often used to provide a pension. It can also be an annual payment for in a will.

Asset

A possession which has value, such as a house, land, cash or securities.

Beneficiary

For inheritance tax purposes, a beneficiary is a person or organisation which receives property, or gets some benefit from, a will, intestacy or trust.

Beneficial joint tenancy

See joint tenancy

Bereaved minor

A person who is aged under 18 and at least one of whose parents or step- parents has died.

Business

For the purpose of business relief, business includes any business carried on n the exercise of a profession or vocation.

Business property

See relevant business property.

Business relief

Relief from Inheritance Tax which is due on a transfer of relevant business property

Chargeable gift

From 22 March 2006, a chargeable gift is, broadly any gift that is not wholly covered by exemptions and given to the trustees of a relevant property trust or a company. Gifts from one individual to another or to disabled person's trust are not chargeable gifts, but are potentially exempt transfers.

Chargeable transfer

A transfer of value made by an individual which is not an exempt transfer.

Chargeable value

The chargeable value of an estate on death is the total of the asset less liabilities less exempt gifts and capital relief.

Charitable trust

A trust which is held indefinitely for charitable purposes only.

Charity exemption

A transfer that is made to a charity or other qualifying body is exempt from inheritance tax.

Chattels

Personal property such as household and personal goods, furniture, jewellery, antiques and works of art, stamp and coin collections, cars, caravans and boats, electrical, clothes, books, and garden equipment.

Consideration

A legal term meaning `something given for something done' i.e. the payment made for goods or services received. For a contract to be valid some consideration must be given.

Confirmation

The process of obtaining a grant of confirmation. In Scotland, England , Wales and Northern Ireland is known as probate .

Deed of Variation

See variation.

Deemed domicile

A legal concept for inheritance tax purposes where a person is treated as if they were domiciled in the UK at the time of a transfer if

- they were domiciled in the UK within three years of the transfer, or
- they were resident in at least 17 of the last 20 years.

Dependant

A dependant of a registered pension scheme is defined as a person who at the time of the scheme member's death was

- the spouse or civil partner of the member
- a child of the member who was under 23
- a child of the member who was over 23 and in opinion of the scheme administrator was dependent on the member
- any other person who in the opinion of the scheme administrator was financially dependent on the member
- had a financial relationship of mutual dependence with member, or was dependent on the member because of physical or mental impairment.

Determination

See notice of determination

Disabled person

For inheritance tax purposes a disabled person is someone who, because of a mental disorder, is not capable of managing their own affairs or administering their own property or someone who is in receipt of attendance allowance or a disability allowance because they are entitled to the care component at the higher or middle rate.

Disabled person's interest

A trust where more than half of the assets in the trust are applied for the benefit of a disabled person. Or, for trusts set up on or after 22 March 2006, a trust set up for their own benefit by a person who is suffering from a condition which can be expected to lead to them becoming disabled.

Discretionary trust

A trust under which no individual has a right to an interest in possession . generally , the trustees have the power to decide who should receive the capital or income from the trust. Discretionary trusts are also relevant property trusts.

Disposition

A disposal or transfer or property or cash, including both the creation and the release of any debt or right. The legislation specifically includes certain types of transfer and more information can be found in the Inheritance Tax Manual.

Domicile

Generally , a person's domicile is where they have their fixed and permanent home and to which, when they are absent, they always have the intention of returning.

Domicile of choice

Where a person has left their country of domicile to live in another country with the intention of settling permanently in the new country.

Domicile of dependency

Under the age of 16 a child has the same domicile as the person on whom they are legally dependent. This is called a domicile of dependency.

Domicile of origin

This is acquired by a child at birth and is usually the domicile of the child's father at that time . It need not be the country in which the child is born.

Donor

A person who makes a gift of some of their assets.

Donee

A person who receives a gift.

Double taxation convention (DTC)

A treaty which helps prevent a transfer from being taxed by two countries if both countries have the right to tax the same property when a death occurs or a gift is made.

Employee trust

A discretionary trust set up to benefit employees of a particular occupation or firm and the relatives and dependants of those employees. For more information on employee trusts, please see our guide – What are special trusts?

Enduring power of attorney

A power of attorney which is not revoked by any subsequent mental incapacity of the person granting the power.

Estate

Up to 22 March 2006, for inheritance tax purposes, a person's estate was made up of :

- assets in the sole name of the deceased,

- their share of any jointly owed assets,
- assets held in a trust in which the deceased had a right to benefit
- any nominated assets, and
- any assets they have given away, but kept an interest in (see gift with reservation) .

From 22 March 2006, a person's estate is made up of

- assets in the sole name of the deceased,
- their share of any jointly owed assets,
- assets held in trust in which the deceased had an immediate post - death interest, a disabled person's interest, or a transitional serial interest.
- Any `nominated assets,' and
- Any assets they have given away, but kept an interest in (see gift with reservation).

the value of an alternatively secured pension fund (ASP) from which the deceased benefited as the original scheme member, or as a dependant who received benefits from the left over ASP fund of the original scheme member. In both cases, the total of all these assets is added to the chargeable value of any gifts made within seven years of the death to work out the amount on which tax is charged.

Excepted asset

An asset on which business relief is not available because it is not used wholly or mainly for the purposes of a business throughout the two years before a transfer. For more information, see the guide on Business Relief.

Excepted estate

An estate where a full inheritance tax account is not required. From 6 April 2004 there are three types of excepted estate:

- low value estates
- except estates
- foreign domiciles

Executor

A man who administers a deceased person's estate in England, Wales and Northern Ireland and is named in the will.

Executor- dative

A man who is appointed by the courts in Scotland to administer a deceased person's estate; usually where there is no will or they are not named in the will.

Executor- nominate

A man who administers a deceased person's estate in Scotland and is named in the will.

Executrices

Plural of executrix.

Executrix

A woman who administers a deceased person's estate in England, Wales and Northern Ireland and is named in the will.

Executrix- dative

A woman who is appointed by the courts in Scotland to administer a deceased person's estate; usually where there is no will or they are not named in the will.

Executrix- nominate

A woman who administers a deceased person's estate in Scotland and is named in the will.

Exempt estate

A type of excepted estate where the gross value of the estate does not exceed £1,000,000 and there can be no liability to inheritance tax because spouse or civil partner exemption or charity exemption bring the estate below the inheritance tax threshold.

Exempt gifts

Gifts that are exempt from inheritance tax. These include

- gifts to individual more than seven years before death. See potentially exempt transfers.
- gifts to spouse or civil partners
- gifts not exceeding £3, 000 in any one tax year. See annual exemption
- gifts on consideration of marriage or civil partnership
- gifts to UK charities
- gifts for national purposes
- small gifts
- gifts which are normal expenditure out of income.

Exempt transfer

An exempt transfer is one that is wholly covered by one or more exemptions.

Exemptions

Some gifts are exempt from inheritance tax because the gifts are covered by exceptions. See exempt gifts for details of the exemptions from inheritance tax which may apply.

Fall in value relief

When tax, or additional tax, is payable on a gift because the donor has died and the value of a gift has fallen between the date of the gift and the death, then tax is usually charged on the reduced value of the gift.

Financial Services Authority (FSA)

The government agency that regulates investment business as required by Financial Services Act 1986.

Gift in consideration of marriage or civil partnership

A gift made to a person who is about to get married or to form a civil partnership . These gifts are exempt from IHT up to the following amounts:

- £5,000 made by the person's parent
- £2,500 made by the person's grandparent
- £1,000 made by anyone else

Gift with reservation

See gift with reservation of benefit.

Gift with reservation of benefit

A gift which is not fully given away so that the person getting the gift does so with conditions attached or the person making the gift keeps back some benefit for themselves.

Grant of confirmation

The proof of legal authority required by the person who is entrusted with dealing with a deceased person's estate in Scotland.

Grant of double probate

A grant of representation where one executor dose not wish to prove the will and the right to join others later is reserved. When the non –proving executor withes to take up office later, a grant of double probate is made. Application for this is made on the form Cap A5C which is available from the Probate and IHT Help line on 0845 3020900.

Grant of representation

The proof of legal authority required by the person who is entrusted with dealing with deceased person's estate.

Grant of letters of administration

The proof of legal authority required by the person who is entrusted with dealing with a deceased person's estate where there is no will, or any will made is invalid.

Grant of letters of administration with will annexed

The proof of legal authority required by the person who is entrusted with dealing with a deceased person's estate where there is a will but no executor is named, or when the executors are unable or unwilling to apply for the grant.

Grant of probate

The proof of legal authority required by the person who is entrusted with dealing with deceased person's estate where there is a will.

Gross value of the estate

The total of all the assets that make up the deceased's estate before any of their debts are taken off.

Her Majesty's Revenue & Customs

The Government department created from the merger of the Inland Revenue and HM Customs & Excise.

ICT

Immediately chargeable transfer

IHT

Inheritance Tax

Immediately chargeable transfer

Before 22March 2006, there was an immediate claim for inheritance tax on gifts into discretionary trusts or to companies. For gifts made on or after 22 March 2006,an immediately chargeable transfer is one made to the trustees of a relevant property trust or to a company. Additional tax may be payable if the donor dies within seven years of the gift.

Immediate post- death interest (IPDI)

The Finance Act 2006 defined an immediate post – death interest (IPDI) as one where a person has an interest in possession in settled property and all the following apply

- the settlement was effected by will or under an intestacy
- the beneficiary became beneficially entitled to the interest in possession on the death of the testator or intestate .

Immovable property

A person's possessions in the form interests in land and the permanent building on the land.

Inheritance Tax

A tax on the value of a person's estate on death and on certain gifts made by an individual during their lifetime.

Inheritance tax threshold

The inheritance tax threshold is the amount above which inheritance tax becomes payable. If the estate, including any assets held in trust and gifts made within seven years of death, is less than the threshold, no inheritance tax will be due on it. See the current threshold .

Interest in possession

This is a term in general law. Generally, a person has an interest in possession in property held in trust if they have the immediate right to use or enjoy the property or receive any income arising from it. Up to 22 March 2006, all such trusts were treated for inheritance tax purposes as owned by the person having the interest in possession. An interest in a trust arising on or after 22 March 2006 will be regarded as an interest in possession (and therefore treated

116

for IHT purposes as owned by the person having an interest in possession) if it is one of the following:

- an immediate post-death interest
- a disabled person's interest
- a transitional serial interest

Intestate

If a person dies intestate, they died without making a will, or without fully disposing of their property by will. The administration of the estate is then governed by the provisions of the Administration of Estates Act 1925.

Intestacy

An estate where the person died intestate.

Inventory

Form C1 Confirmation with inventory is the form used for a Scottish estate on which the person's representative has to provide information such as assets of the estate, including assets situated outside of Scotland.

Joint asset

See joint property

Joint property

Something that is jointly owned by two or more people either as a 'joint tenancy' or as 'tenants in common'. Find out more about joint property in our guide to passing on your home to your children.

Joint tenancy

A form of joint ownership where all the joint owners have an identical interest in the property. On the death of the one owner, their interest passes to the remaining owner(s) by survivorship.

Life interest

A common form of interest in possession in settled property where a person has an interest for the duration of their lifetime.

Life tenant

A person who holds a life interest in settled property .

Limited probate

Where an executor is appointed in respect of certain assets only, such as literary works.

Loss to the estate

The value of a gift for inheritance tax purposes is the amount of the loss to the estate. It is worked out by looking at the value of the estate before and after the gift was made.

The difference between those two figures is the loss in the estate.

Low value estates

A type of except estate where there can be no liability to inheritance tax because the total value of the estate, including the deceased's share of jointly owned assets, any specified transfer and specified exempt transfer, does not exceed the inheritance tax threshold .

Maintenance funds for historic lands & buildings

A type of discretionary trust set up for the maintenance of designated lands and buildings. Relief from full discretionary trust charges is available for these funds, but tax charge may arise if any property ceases to be held on the relevant trusts, or when the trustees make a disposition which reduces the value of the trusts.

Movable property

Goods, furniture and other items which can be moved from place to place.

National purposes

Exemption from inheritance tax is given for gifts and bequests to certain national institutions such as the National Gallery.

Newspaper trusts

Trusts set up for newspaper publishing companies or newspaper holding companies. These are treated like employee trusts for inheritance tax purposes.

Nil-rate band

The amount of an estate on which there is no inheritance tax to pay. If the value of an estate, including any assets held in trust and gifts made within seven years of death, falls within the nil – rate band there will be no IHT payable on the estate. Where the value of an estate exceeds the nil – rate band, only the amount above the nil – rate band is taxed at 40%.

Nominated asset

Certain assets, such as deposits with Friendly societies, National Savings Bank accounts and National Savings Certificates, can be transferred on death direct to chosen beneficiaries by nomination. Nominated property does not pass under the will or intestacy but it does form a part of the estate for inheritance tax purposes.

Nominee

A person who holds property on behalf of another.

Normal expenditure out of income

Gifts which are made purely out of income as part of a person's normal expenditure are exempt from inheritance tax. The claimant must show that after allowing for the gifts the donor was left with sufficient income to maintain their usual standard of living and that there was an established pattern of giving.

Notice of determination

A notice of determination may be issued where the personal representatives do not agree the value of the transfer.

It is a written notice which states that the outstanding matters have been determined or payment of the outstanding tax has not been made. There is a right to appeal.

Open market value

For inheritance tax, the open market value of an asset is the price it might reasonably fetch if it was sold on the open market at the time of the transfer of that asset.

Outright gift

A gift where the donor gives away full ownership of the gift and does not retain any benefit.

Pecuniary legacy

A gift of a sum of money under a will.

Permanent home

The country where a person intends to live for the remainder of their life. It is the country whose laws decide, for example, whether a Will is valid, or how the estate of a person who has not made a Will is dealt with when they die.

Per stirpes

A property is to be divided 'per stirpes' among the children of a deceased person, then each child takes an equal share. If a child has predeceased and the deceased that child's children will take equally between them the share that the predeceased child would have taken.

Personal applicant

A person who is applying for a grant of representation without the help of a solicitor or other agent.

PET

See potentially exempt transfer.

Political party

A gift to a political party qualifies to exemption from the inheritance tax if at the last general election preceding the transfer either two members of the party were elected to the House of Commons, or one member of the party was so elected and not less than 150,000 votes were given to candidates who were members of that party.

Potentially exempt transfer

Up to 22 March 2006, a potentially exempt transfer (PET) was an outright gift to an individual, to an accumulation and maintenance trust, or to a disabled person's interest, which becomes an exempt transfer if the donor lives for seven years after the date of the gift.

Power of attorney

An authority given by one person to another to act for him in their absence. The person authorised to act is the attorney of the other. See also enduring power of attorney.

Privileged will

A will made by a soldier on active service or a sailor at sea which does not have to comply with the usual formalities to make it valid. It does not have to be in writing, or, if it is in writing, does not have to be witnessed by two witnesses. The soldier or sailor can also be a minor.

Probate

Strictly, the exhibiting and proving of a will by the executors. In common usage as a general term describe the process of obtaining a grant of representation.

Property

The word 'property' for inheritance tax purposes includes all types of asset, cash, stocks and shares etc as well as land and buildings, including all rights and interest of any description that are legally enforceable.

Proportionate charge

An inheritance tax charge on a relevant property trust (link to relevant property trust in the glossary) which arises when property in the trust ceases to be relevant property or when the trustees make a disposition   which reduces the value of the relevant property.

The main example of property ceasing to be relevant property are when the settlement comes to an end or when some of the property is distributed to beneficiaries.

Quick succession relief

See successive charges relief.

Related property

Related property is property that is in the estate of a spouse or civil partner, or belonging to a charity or one of the political, national or public bodies to which exempt transfers may be made. There are special rules for valuing related property.

Related settlement

When a settlor sets up a trust, any other trust he sets up on the same day are related settlements.

Relevant business property

Types of property on which business relief may be available. These include

- a business
- an interest in a Business, such as a partner
- unquoted shares which are not listed on recognised stock exchange
- shares or securities which give the transferor control of a business
- land, buildings, plant or machinery used wholly or mainly in the business or partnership

Relevant dependant

A relevant dependant of a member of a registered pension scheme is someone who at the date of the scheme member's death was

- a dependant who was the person's spouse or civil partner or
- is financially dependant on the member at the time.

Relevant property

Settled property held on a relevant property trust.

Relevant property trust

From 22 March 2006, a relevant property trust is any trust in which the beneficiary's interest is not one of the following:

- an immediate post – death interest
- a transitional serial interest
- a disabled person's interest

- a trust for a bereaved minor
- an age 18 to 25 trust

Relievable property
Property on which business relief or agricultural relief is available.

Resident
For inheritance tax purposes, residence has the same meaning as for income tax purposes. To be regarded as resident in the UK you must normally be physically present in the country at same time in the tax year.

You will always be resident if you are here for 183 days or more in the tax year.

Residue
The part of an estate which is left after the payment of specific and pecuniary legacies, debts, funeral expenses and IHT.

Restriction on disposal
The value of an asset may be reduced if the right to dispose of it is restricted.

Reversionary Interest
The future right to an interest in settled property.
Settlement
A settlement occurs when property is held in trust for successive beneficiaries . The property which a settlor puts into trust is known as the trust fund or` settled property'.

Settlor

A person who puts property into trust. For inheritance tax purposes a settlor is the person who makes a settlement or who directly or indirectly provides the assets for a settlement.

Simultaneous deaths

For inheritance tax, if two or more people die and it is not known who died first, we assume that they have died at the same moment. This does not alter the legal position for the administration of the estate which is that the elder is presumed to have died first.

Small gifts

Small gifts which are exempt from inheritance tax of up to £250 in each tax year to any number of different recipients. The exemption cannot be combined with any other exemption such as the annual exemption.

Special Commissioners

The Special Commissioners hear and determine appeals concerning decisions of the Inland Revenue relating to all direct taxes including income tax, corporation tax, capital gains tax and inheritance tax.

Special Trust

Types of discretionary trusts where the settled property held on them is not relevant property.

Special gifts

A gift other than a gift of residue Typical specific gifts are pecuniary legacies, gifts of particular assets such as the deceased's residence, furniture, jewellery and other household and personal goods and effects or shares in companies and business assets.

Specified exempt transfers

Gifts other than the deceased's spouse or civil partner   charities, political parties, housing associations, maintenance funds for historic buildings and employee trusts must be added back to see if the estate qualifies as an excepted estate.

Specified transfers

Gifts of cash, chattels or corporeal movables, quoted shares or securities, or outright gifts of land or buildings to individuals, not gifts into trust.

For an estate to qualify as excepted estate (excepted estate), specified transfer made within 7 days of death cannot exceed £100,000.

Spouse

A person who is legally married to someone else.

Spouse or civil partner exemption

Gifts made between spouses or civil partners are exempt from inheritance tax. This exemption is limited to £55, 000 if the deceased (or donor) was domiciled in the UK and their spouse or civil partner was not domiciled in the UK at time of the transfer.

Successive charges relief

A relief designed to reduce the burden of IHT where an estate taxable on death reflects the benefit of property received within the previous five years under a transfer on which tax was (or becomes) payable. Calculation of the relief is shown in the article- Tell me how to calculate successive charges relief.

Surviving civil partner

A person whose civil partnership has ended through death of their civil partner.

Survivorship

Where property is owned jointly under a joint tenancy, on the death of one of the joint tenants, the deceased's share of the joint property passes automatically to the surviving joint tenant(s). The property cannot be passed to anyone else under a will or intestacy.

Taper relief

If the total chargeable value of all the gifts made between three and seven years before death is more than the threshold at death, then taper relief is due. The relief reduces the amount of tax payable on a gift, not the value of the gift itself.

Ten – yearly charge

An inheritance tax charge which arises on a relevant property trust on the tenth anniversary of the setting up of the trust and each subsequent ten- yearly anniversary.

Tenancy in common

See tenants in common.

Tenants in common

Joint ownership of property where each joint tenant owns a separate share in the property. On the death of one of the joint owners, their share passes to their beneficiaries by their will or intestacy. There is more on joint property in Passing on your home to your children.

Testator
A man who has made a will.

Testatrix
A woman who has made a will.

Transfer
Inheritance tax is charged on a transfer of value. That transfer can occur either during a person's lifetime, in the form of a gift, or on a person's death.

Transferee
A person who receives a transfer.

Transferor
A person who make a transfer.

Trust
An obligation binding a person who holds the legal title, the trustee, to deal with the property for the benefit of another person; the beneficiary

Trust fund
See settlement

Trustee
The person who holds the legal title to settled property   and who is obliged to deal with the property for the benefit of the beneficiaries.

Trust for a bereaved minor

A trust for a bereaved minor is a trust which is exempt from mainstream inheritance tax charges if it is held either

- on the statutory trust applying to minor children aged up to 18 on intestacy or
- on trusts in similar terms established under the terms of a parent's will or by the Criminal Injuries Compensation Scheme.

Trust for disabled people

A discretionary trust set up for the benefit of a disabled person. After 9 March 1991 these trust were treated as if the disabled person had an interest in possession in the property held in the trust. Any distributions from the trust to the disabled person are not taxable, but a charge to IHT will arise on their death and the trust fund will form part of their estate.

Unilateral Relief

Where a transfer is liable to Inheritance Tax and also to similar tax imposed by another country on assets situated in that country with which the UK does not have a double taxation agreement, relief may be available under unilateral relief provisions.

Variation

If all of the original beneficiaries agree, an inheritance under a will or under an intestacy can be changed after death.

Will

The legal document by which a person declares their intention as to what should happen to their estate after their death.

Woodlands relief

When a woodland in the United Kingdom is transferred on death, the person who would be liable for the tax can elect to have the value of the trees and under wood (but not underlying land) excluded from the deceased's estate. If the timber is later disposed of its value at the time will be subject to inheritance tax.

****

Index

****

www.straightforwardco.co.uk

All titles, listed below, in the Straightforward Guides Series can be purchased online, using credit card or other forms of payment by going to www.straightfowardco.co.uk A discount of 25% per title is offered with online purchases.

Law

A Straightforward Guide to:

Consumer Rights

Bankruptcy Insolvency and the Law

Employment Law

Private Tenants Rights

Family law

Small Claims in the County Court

Contract law

Intellectual Property and the law

Divorce and the law

Leaseholders Rights

The Process of Conveyancing

Knowing Your Rights and Using the Courts

Producing Your own Will

Housing Rights

The Bailiff the law and You

Probate and The Law

Company law

What to Expect When You Go to Court

Guide to Competition Law

Give me Your Money-Guide to Effective Debt Collection

Caring for a Disabled Child

General titles

Letting Property for Profit

Buying, Selling and Renting property

Buying a Home in England and France

Bookkeeping and Accounts for Small Business

Creative Writing

Freelance Writing

Writing Your own Life Story

Writing performance Poetry

Writing Romantic Fiction

Speech Writing

Teaching Your Child to Read and write

Teaching Your Child to Swim

Raising a Child-The Early Years

Creating a Successful Commercial Website

The Straightforward Business Plan

The Straightforward C.V.

Successful Public Speaking

Handling Bereavement

Play the Game-A Compendium of Rules

Individual and Personal Finance

Understanding Mental Illness

The Two Minute Message

Guide to Self Defence

Buying a Used Car

Tiling for Beginners

Go to:

www.straightforwardco.co.uk